We Were Cold Warriors Volume 3.

Swing that lamp...

Also by Jonno DP on Amazon

We Were Cold Warriors. (Published June 2019)

We Were Cold Warriors Volume 2. (Published December 2020)

Reviews on volume 2 (mostly from Amazon)

I initially read the intro and was surprised at how daft all three Services can be when its written down on paper. You tend to think it's just ... (Insert, "Arm, Corp, Regt, Sqn, Sect, Mates or You")
Some very good "dits" that did make me laugh out loud properly. Very much enjoyed reading this.

We can all relate to this utter Tomfoolery! Jonno has touched on a little gem here; he's put on to paper what us vets and serving talk about years later; we may not talk for a decade but when we get together again, it's 'Do you remember...?" Genius idea and a great read.

A collection of tales that will make you laugh till the tears run down your trouser leg. My favourite is the waving from the train.

It's a great book, some hilarious true stories in there so big credit to the author. Would highly recommend to all ex-military with that 'special' sense of humour!!

...please, please let there be a Volume 3!

Brought back so many memories of a more innocent time.

Jonno DP grew up (well, got older) near Bodmin in Cornwall. (The then murder capital of the UK – the only distinction Bodmin has ever had) He took the shilling at 15 and three quarters and started basic training as a Junior Leader in September 1980, just after his sixteenth birthday and wondered what hit him.

After a decade playing silly buggers in the Royal Artillery and reaching the dizzying heights of Bombardier he got out after The Wall fell thinking it would all go quiet and be a bit boring. That is, just before Gulf 1, Kosovo, Bosnia, Sierra Leone, Afghanistan, and Gulf 2.

After a few years doing various unsatisfying jobs, he studied for, and got, (well, scraped to be honest) a degree in Maths and Physics. He now spends five days a week in a secondary school teaching teenagers who don't give a fuck how many beans make four. He can't wait to retire and write full time.

Jonno DP in 2022 aged 57 and a bit.

This book is dedicated to the brave people of Ukraine. Especially Roman Hrybov, the Ukrainian border guard on Snake Island who, on the 24th of February 2022, told the Russian flagship Moskva to "Go fuck yourselves!"

The Ukrainian stamp commemorating the fuck off.

Why I wrote this book.

Book one was just a laugh, (but boy did it take off!), book two was because I had so many stories left over from book one, and by the time I had finished with that I STILL had loads left over. At the time of writing this, I am locked down because of covid and bored and there are few better ways of spending a damp Sunday than enjoying stories of people who served.
When I was in the army I used to wonder how I ended up in a battery of such odd people. After a bit I realised the whole regiment was filled with odd people, and then I found out that some people in other regiments were even odder... I started to realise that this was just the beginning... and the RAF and Navy are just the same. It makes me giggle to think that in a thousand years historians might read these tales, shake their head and say the thirty first century equivalent of, 'What the fuck is wrong with these people?' And until the end of time YOU were one of those people! I salute you, you magnificent bastards!
I must admit though, I harboured a lingering suspicion that the people currently serving were a bit, how can I put this... a bit more normal than previous generations. Then in June 2021 I moved house to a little town called Calne in Wiltshire and found myself living opposite Josh Fox who is a recy mech in the REME. He is 32, so quite a lot younger than my 57 and a bit, and often asks rude questions. One day I showed him an ancient flintlock pistol that I had bought from an antiques dealer intending to hang it up on a wall somewhere. He gazed at it for a moment then asked, "Was that your personal weapon when you were in?" In return I express surprise at every possible opportunity that the army trusts him and his REME colleagues with real guns and live ammunition. He has told me some belting tales that I will publish when I have the necessary permissions but his Yorkshire accent (I refer to it as

his speech defect) is sometimes a cause for confusion. One day we were in his back garden splitting a crate and he mentioned an exercise where he spent the night in a muddy hall.
"What did you do that for?" I asked.
He looked at me as if I was simple. "Didn't you ever spend the night in a muddy hall?"
"No."
"How long were you in?"
"Ten years."
"And in ten years you never spent the night in a muddy hall?"
"No. I was in a normal unit that was outside."
He stared at me for a moment figuring out what had gone wrong with the conversation. I saw his expression change as he realised what the problem was.
"HALL." He said louder as if increased volume would help.
"HALL! A muddy HALL! H – O – L – E! HALL!"
"HOLE!" I said, "Its pronounced **HOLE**, not **HALL**! You Yorkshiremen need to spend more time learning to speak properly and less time playing fucking cricket."
"And you Cornishmen need to clean your ears out and stop fucking sleeping with your sister."
This is how I spend my summer evenings.
In one of the earlier volumes, I mentioned that if you go back to the second world war the mentality of the British Military was the same and it started me thinking, 'When did this start?'
There is no doubt that the British generally are weird compared to other nationalities, and so maybe this is the root of the 'Squaddie mentality' and its RAF and RN equivalent.
Bill Bryson, the witty American writer and lover of all things British once commented on our unusual attitude to life. He suggested that if you got two strangers from say, Germany, France, or in fact any European nation and put them in a train carriage together, they may talk to each other, but they will do no more. If you put two Brits that don't know each other

together you will be able to tell they are Brits because within five minutes they will make each other laugh.

Weird when you think about it. Why do we have this compulsion to amuse one another? – even strangers that we will probably never see again.

I do the same and always have done as far as I can remember, but I couldn't actually explain *why* I do it, and trust me, my wife has often asked.

I sometimes wonder if I would keep my instinct to amuse if I was in serious shit. I have read lots of accounts of British military cracking jokes under fire and I found a particular gem whilst doing research for this book. It was an eighties era clip on YouTube made by the army and was called, 'The Falklands War – The Land Battle Part 3 - The Final Battle'. It was interesting to watch, very 1980s. All the officers had plummy accents and all the NCOs looked uncomfortable. (Odd that loads of them had MMs etc for bravery in battle and looked like they would rather do it again than say their piece to camera). I know the army is very different these days, I have a mate who joined after me as a gunner and is a full colonel now. (By the way, he might be a colonel, but he's still a NIG.) Anyway, thirty-seven minutes in Major JP Kiszely MC from the Scots Guards was explaining that his company had been pinned down during the attack on Tumbledown for over half an hour with the temperature well below zero. It was so cold that men were starting to go down with exposure and some unconscious soldiers were being dragged back down the hill and casevaced. He was lying next to his signaller, and they were both shivering, but (his words), "Our inhibitions wouldn't allow us to have bodily contact." Finally, they decided that it was so cold that it was a case of get together and share body heat or become a casualty. Whilst they were in this friendly position (and still under fire remember) the signaller said in his cockney accent, "Ey sir, wot they gonna fink if we're both killed and they find our bodies like this?"

The British military also seem to have balls of steel if they see an opportunity to crack a funny gag, even if the repercussions could be nasty. I was once told a story, probably apocryphal, about a soldier on parade and the Sergeant Major was less than impressed with his turnout. The Sergeant Major jabbed him in the chest with his pace stick and roared, "There's shit on the end of this stick!" The object of his wrath looked down at the point lodged between his ribs, looked back up at the Sarnt Major and replied, "It's alright my end sir." Oh, I pray every night that that story is true.

Or another, that I would love to find out is true (so email me at damonjohnson@zoho.com if you know anything) is a story that the CO of the 1st Battalion Scots Guards, Sir Gregor McGregor (do you think he might be Scottish?) was riding a horse on parade when his mount let go a world beating fart. "Sorry about that Brigade of Drums." he called.

"That's all right sir." replied a piper. "We thought it was the horse." Like I said, balls of steel.

The other thing that occurred to me during my research was that the British often live in extremes of tolerance and aggression. The British people are polite to a fault, and will go out of their way to not fall out with people, but once they lose their rag... well...

This has translated into the fearsome reputation that British forces have. Great peacekeepers, but once those forces are aimed and the trigger is pulled they win battles and wars that they really shouldn't have. I did research as far back as the Crimean War (yes, we invaded Russia once) and I found out about The Charge of the Light Brigade in 1854. The Light Brigade was a cavalry unit that attacked some Russian artillery at the end of a long valley that was blasting away at them as quickly as they could load their guns. These Russian guns also had infantry support on both sides of the valley that was able to fire down into it. Incredibly, there is no record whatsoever of any objection being raised by anyone of any rank even though the enemy positions, guns and infantry, were clearly visible to them before they attacked.

In a way it's not such a surprise that such events happened. Historians estimate that at one time or another Britain has invaded 60% of all the countries that exist today. If you add on the ones we have colonised and the ones we have regarded as hostile territory (for example Norway during WW2) it's hard to think of any at all that we haven't gone after with a big stick. So once again you sick puppies, pull up a sandbag, swing the lamp, and make yourself comfortable. Here is another instalment of the stuff that never made it into the history books.

Oh, and should you feel so inclined, email me at damonjohnson@zoho.com to get yourself into book 4!

No good deed goes unpunished

It was a cold and snowy winter night probably late 2013 (but it's hard to be sure after all the alchohol I consumed during my time in Germany) when my friend and I were stumbling through the German town of Gutersloh after a merry evening of drinks looking for a taxi to take us back to camp. The taxi rank was only a few hundred metres away, but it seemed much further. Like all good soldiers, we were adequately dressed for the snowy weather (jeans and T shirts) and with our faces tucked as low as possible we marched quickly towards the taxi rank by the train station. On rounding a corner we stopped dead. There was a body lying face down on the freezing pavement. After a quick 5s and 20s we were satisfied no mugger was around and moved closer. It was a young bloke wearing only a white T-shirt and red chinos and I knew he wouldn't survive the night if left alone. Using the medical knowledge we had both gained on a recent First Aid course we discussed the case briefly and agreed on a diagnosis. Shitfaced. We rolled him onto his back and, as per BLS, gave him the shake, shout, response treatment. We laughed as he slurred complaints at us. "What's your name mate?" I asked.
"Hector." He grumbled, trying to roll back over and return to the land of nod.
"He must be one of the loggies from our camp." I said.
My mate nodded. "Yeah, I reckon so."
"Come on, we'll just take him back to camp with us; saves us pissing around with the plod all night." We hefted him onto legs made of jelly and I pulled his arm over my shoulder. My friend tucked his shoulder under Hectors. Closer, but better to take the weight. We started lift/dragging him towards the nearby taxi rank.
The doors on our chosen vehicle slammed shut and we were away toward Princess Royal Barracks. My mate and I were up

front and Hector was in the back, snoozing. After a bit a really rancid pong started to become noticeable. "Have you farted?' I asked.
"No!" He snapped back having been thinking it was me. We both glanced at the driver who just grunted and shook his head.
"Well where the... oh fuck, no..." he said as he sniffed his hand. "No no, no, no, you've got the be fucking KIDDING me!" I laughed until I felt sick as we discovered my mates entire left side was covered in shit, whereas I was clean. I leant back to have a look at Hector and in the light of the passing streetlamps I saw his back was caked with shit. I laughed and thought 'dirty bastard.' As time passed the smell became worse and worse until it became unbearable. I think the volcano was still erupting if you know what I mean. This choking fog of stink filled the confined space even with the windows down but finally to our great relief the gates and patrolling guards came into view. I got out trying not to notice the fuming taxi driver while my mate stood to the side surveying the damage to his clothes. I pulled the back door open and said loudly, "Out!" Hector shook his head and grumbled. "Now!" I ordered, louder, but still he didn't move. Getting a bit pissed off by now I grabbed one wrist and one ankle and dragged him out of the taxi and onto the ground. "Get up!" No response. Hector was lying on a wet road amongst grit, salt and assorted crap but was too pissed to care.
He was having none of it, but neither was I. "Fuck it, fine then." I grabbed both his ankles and dragged him towards the guard room, his head bouncing around like a ping pong ball on the road. I heaved the uncooperative shitstain into the guardroom and told the wide-eyed Guard Commander to, "Get the fucking monkeys out here."
"Oh my god." A young soldier said as she gagged. "Has he shit himself?"

"Mate," My friend said leaning through the door. "The taxi man's fucking raging."
"Have you paid him?"
"Yeah, but he's charging a cleaning bill. He's not happy."
HE'S not happy! Oh right! I carefully dug into Hector's pockets avoiding the klingons but only found his Sparkasse bank card. Shit!
Literally and figuratively...
I went into the back of the guard room and grabbed some blue roll and soap and went out to the taxi. The driver was waving his hands and making noises I pretended not to hear as my mate and I scrubbed his seats. Task finished, he was told to fuck off and unhappily, still pouring out various threats, he complied.
By now the guardroom contained some Military Police. The three of them stood there with their standard issue dumbfounded expression as they eyed Hector who lay on the floor with turned out pockets absolutely caked in it. The monkeys gave me a suspicious 'You nicked his fucking wallet didn't you!' look.
With a weary sigh and the long night grinding me down I handed Clouseau the bank card we found on Hector and drew a breath. "We found him lying in the street like this sparked out on booze. We figured he was a loggie and brought him back before he died of exposure. Now he's your problem, good night." My friend and I left Hector to the tender care of the monkeys and went to our accommodation where I took a hot shower and fell into my pit.
A few weeks later, I was booking out of the guardroom when the young soldier who had been gagging on the smell that night approached me pointing her finger and grinning. "It's you!" she beamed. I somehow doubted she found my broken nose and general complexion attractive, or had mistaken me for Hugh Grant, so I figured it must be in regard to Hector.

"Did the monkeys square that complete weapon away?" I asked.
"Kind of." She giggled.
"What the hell's that meant to mean?"
Her amusement at that night swelled my concern. "Well…. erm….. his mum was really grateful you looked after him."
"What's his fucking mum got to do with this?"
"Well, you know how he was a loggie from this camp?"
A horrible feeling of realisation came over me… "Uh…. Yeahhhh…."
"Well, he wasn't. It turns out that technically you kidnapped a local national. His Mum came and picked him up the following day when he woke up in our jail. But she doesn't want you arrested or anything…"
"Oh… uh…. that's good" I heard myself saying. I am fucking leaving the next one…

Cpl Johnson AAC, Princess Royal Bks, 2013.

"DON'T PUSH THE BUTTONS..... ARE YOU LISTENING TO ME????"

Whilst at 30 Signal Regiment in Bramcote I was sent out to Kosovo as the Foreman of Signals to oversee a HQ move with the Gurkha Signal Squadron. There had been a load of rioting in Podevo, North of Pristina and a Dutch Regiment had been battered by the Kosovan rioters. Their CO had locked the regiment in its barracks and was refusing to let his soldiers go out as long as there were rioters about so the RRF sent a Company (yep, just one company) up to Podevo and quelled most of the riots in 2 days or so. Four of us SNCOs wanted to do a bit of military tourism so we harangued Craig, the MT Staff Sergeant at the HQ to let us take the Generals spare armoured Range Rover as he was on leave and we wanted to check out how good the riots were. Finally he gave in but as we were about to set off, he said "Whatever you do, don't use any of the buttons in the centre console!".
Hmmmm...
There were three red buttons, numbered 1, 2 and 3, and 2 others labelled Lights and Siren. We thought no more of it! The rioting wasn't that good, the Fusiliers had done their job well, so it was a bit of a wasted trip. On the way back, I think it was Brendan who was the first to press one of the buttons. Smoke billowed out of the vehicle and completely engulfed the folk standing at the side of the road. We drove off and it was decided that we should all have a go, to save one person getting completely in the shit. I mean there were two Sergeants, a Staff Sergeant and a WO2!
You have to remember that it wasn't that long after the fighting had been significantly reduced in Kosovo and occasional incidents were still happening. So, when we got to a set of traffic lights in a village, it was up to each passenger to pop the buttons. First a set of flash-bangs erupted, followed closely by

CS gas. Folk were diving all over the place, taking cover and then choking and rubbing their eyes. We thought it was probably time to leave, so the blue lights and sirens went on and we peeled away from the lights which were still on red. Upon our return, we handed the vehicle back to Craig who could immediately tell what had happened by the sheepish way we entered his office. "You cunts pressed the fucking buttons didn't you?"

We shuffled our feet like naughty schoolboys and avoided eye contact. "Errrmmm...... sorry."

"It's gonna cost ten grand to re-arm the defensive suite, you lot owe me BIG time!"

In exchange for our two-tins-a-night beer ration for a month Craig put in a vehicle fault report blaming the electrics. This meant Craig was the owner of 10 cans a night for a whole month!

On the same deployment, I was responsible for the technical deployment of the HQ, including the power. The electrician, a Ghurkha called Prem approached me.

"FofS" (short for Foreman of Signals), "I have to go APOD and service genny."

"OK Prem." I said, "Have you done the genny here?"

"Yes FofS."

"Done the oil & filters?"

"Yes FofS."

"The diesel has been filled up?"

"Yes FofS."

"All we have to do is start it and switch over the Lewden box?"

"Yes FofS."

"Cracking Prem, let me know when you get to the APOD."

"Yes FofS." Prem jumps in his rover and off he tootles to service the generator at the APOD. No sooner had his vehicle left the camp and the dust settles than the gennie stopped.

The chief of staff called, "FOREMAAAAN!!!!!! Where's the bloody power????" Prem hadn't done anything I had asked

him, so there I am with a couple of others running backwards and forwards, diesel in, start up and get the power back on.
Then I got a call from the APOD. "Prem, you said you had done everything on the genny!"
"Yes FofS."
"You'd done nothing, we lost power and I got a bollocking off the CoS"
"Yes FofS."
I handed the phone to my trusty Sergeant, a lovely bloke called Surrendra. "Surrendra, see what Prem says, tell him I'm not fucking happy!"
Surrendra takes the phone, there is lots of Nepali, Surrendra gets annoyed and raises his voice a bit. Not shouting, but I can tell by the tone he's tearing a strip off Prem. He puts the phone down.
"So why did Prem tell me everything was sorted?"....
"He was too frightened to say no to you, so he just said 'Yes FofS' to everything!"
Ghurkhas, gotta love 'em.

Gaz Duffy, Royal Signals (1985-2010)

"There's lost, and then there's 2nd Lieutenant lost."
Anon

Second breakfast, yum yum

In the late 60s, I drove home from Germany for a week's leave in the North of England, after which I was to attend a four-week course in the South. As I left my parents' home to go to the course, my mother (as mothers do) gave me a bag of sandwiches and a thermos flask, full of minestrone soup.
I arrived at the barracks in the late evening and was given a room in an annexe to the Sergeants Mess which contained six single rooms and a central washroom with three showers, three cubicles and three wash basins. I was the first occupant to arrive.
The next morning, before breakfast, I decided to take the flask to the dining room and fill it with tea. It was still full of the soup so took it into the washroom and emptied it into one of the basins but, unfortunately, it did not drain away but lay there like a giant technicolour yawn, blocking the basin. As I was the only occupant of the block, I decided to deal with it after breakfast by bringing a spoon back with me and poking it through the holes.
Unfortunately, the cleaner beat me to it and I returned to find her in the washroom, gazing in horror and rage at the multicoloured pile of carrots and peas. Before I got a chance to explain, she began a tirade of foul-mouthed language, accusing me of all sorts of bad behaviour, but concentrating on how disgusting I was to puke in a sink and leave it there. Now, I don't know about you, but I have had most words thrown at me during my career, but I learnt some new ones that morning, which annoyed me.
So, I took the spoon, lifted a spoonful of the offending pile, ate it, and said, "It can't have been there long; it's still warm!" I then offered her a spoonful!

The resulting scream rivalled a fire alarm, with the Doppler Effect showing as she fled out of the building and was followed by the sound of loud retching.
Following a short interview with the RSM, it was decided that for the rest of the course I would be cleaning my own room!

Harry F.

Hide and seek in the army

22 Signal regiment around 1985 or 1986. The long-awaited trip to Vogelsang for battle camp was kicked off by the longest train journey in the world as we were shunted from siding to siding to allow regular train services past. We had been told that there would be a large-scale escape and evasion exercise for the regiment at the beginning of the camp which made an interesting departure from the normal routine in the Royal Signals, that is 'Getting in, establishing comms and keeping comms up.' The infantry stuff was a 'now and again' thing and made a welcome change. It's fair to say there was some excitement as well as some blokes were determined to outwit the DS on the escape and evasion phase. Many Deutschmarks were spent on gadgets supplied by BCB and Survival Aids, and many amateur barrack room tailors stitched items into obscure areas of kit. Also, everyone had a team they were going to 'run with'.

Part way into the trip the train stops next to a large meadow, nowhere near a station. This was not an unusual occurrence; on trains we were often shunted into sidings for long periods for no known reason. But this time it was different, the DS descended upon us and got us all off the train. And rather than line us up by squadron and troop they launched a massive game of murder ball. We were having a great time but unbeknownst to us they were picking random bodies out and bussing them away in closed up bedfords. So that part of our plan, sticking in a team, had been foiled right at the start!
After we were nabbed we were taken to a weather-beaten German hill with a barbed wire holding pen big enough for the entire regiment. We were processed with the usual things that happen on an E&E exercise when caught, stripped, cold water dowsing, interrogated, and numbered (across the forehead

with engineers blue!). Once through and dressed in most of our kit (some confiscations to make life interesting), we were put in four internal
quadrants in the holding pen. There was an aisle down the middle and a crosswalk in line with an oddly placed 12x12 in the middle. The Regiment had made an attempt to make the exercise feel authentic. There were guards wandering around in Russian greatcoats carrying rubber AK47s.

I was stood right next to the tent on the front row of the rear half of the troops, facing the crosswalk. Throughout the many hours it took to process the rest of the Regiment, the medics had been getting a quadrant at a time to run on the spot to stay warm. Suddenly an order was shouted for us all to run on the spot. The guards were looking confused and as I looked around, I noticed two guys at the far end of my row, running towards me. They had given the order as cover and were heading for 'my' 12x12! Every time they passed someone, they joined in. Sometimes, (not often, but sometimes) I can think quickly and on this occasion I did. I darted past the poor guy with the Russian great coat and rubber AK and got to the rear door.

I felt a bit sorry for the poor bloke doing the guarding to be honest. He was suddenly confronted with the entire regiment running at him and nothing to defend himself with except a rubber assault rifle. I don't know if he had the sense to get out of the way or whether he got trampled by a stampeding herd of signallers, ending up with many a boot print shaped bruise!

I was at the front desperately trying to undo the fucking toggles on the tent with fingers stiff with cold and the entire regiment at my back building up the pressure and making it harder. I finally got enough of the toggles undone and I was spat out like a cherry pip followed by everyone else swearing and yelling and shooting off in every direction. We didn't know where we were, none of us had a plan or a map and we didn't know what the endex rules were. I distinctly remember the WO1 Training Officer (WO1 Cartwright I think), clambering onto the roof of one of the Bedfords shouting "STOP! THE FUCKING EXERCISE HASN'T STARTED YET!!..."

As you can imagine there were some choice phrases launched in his direction!
I chose to go solo for a bit and did some running along rivers, middle of roads etc to defeat search dogs. (Get me!) Dodging in and out of gardens, through the woods etc. Eventually I hooked up with a couple of other guys and we spent a couple of uncomfortable nights moving around, seeking shelter, trying to sleep in the cold. At one point we found ourselves sneaking through a village with a schnellie. Between us we managed to sneak some cash through the searches, and I was nominated to dash across and buy some food. What a sight I must have made, sweaty, dirty combats, blue number on my head and dodgy German language skills. (If it wasn't "Noch zwei biers!" I was reduced to pointing!). Halfway through cooking a couple of bratties mit pommes, (all we could afford), I suddenly heard the distinctive sound of land rover tyres pulling up outside and the tinny thunk of doors closing behind the hunter force. Time to do one! I demanded of the woman behind the counter if there was a back door. She obliged and I scarpered sharpish. I'd gotten away by the skin of my teeth.
After a lengthy bout of fence hopping and ditch running I hooked up with my oppos again and we went back in to recover our probably cold schnellie. That wonderful woman provided free of charge a massive feed that stood us in good stead for pretty much the rest of the escape!
We finally figured out where we were, as one of the guys had been to Vogelsang before, and he was able to navigate us back in to find out what the hell was happening. We got in to camp and were directed to the Ops room where the adjutant was waiting for us. He congratulated us, gave us a brief on how to get to the finish line then said, "You have to the count of ten before I send the hunter force looking for you."

We just looked at him.
"One, two, three..."
He got no further, we were off!
Eventually after three days we managed to get everyone back in camp and found we had inadvertently got revenge for the sneaky tricks played on us by the training staff. We had missed two days where we should have been on the ranges. Escape and evasion and range days don't mix well!

Frank McGoldrick, Royal Signals

A blue and white day

You know that old saying, The Army Made a Man of Me? In my case I actually remember the moment when it happened. I was 16 years old and doing my basic training at Junior Leaders Regiment Royal Artillery at Bramcote near Nuneaton. There were twenty troops there and all of them had to spend a week doing adventure training in Wales at some point in the year. Some jammy bastards got their week in the summer, we got February.

It was a long, long, cold, cold ride in the back of bedfords and at the end of it we climbed out the back of the truck to gaze upon the 'facilities'. We all had that stiff and painful muscle feeling you get when you have had to be still for a long time when you are really cold. (Remember that?) We jumped out and landed in snow that went halfway up our shins. This unhappy start was offset by the picturesque and snug looking cottage to our right. Someone we didn't recognise was leaning against the doorframe drinking a brew with one hand and scratching his testicles with the other.

"Not toooo bad." Muttered someone next to me.

"Fuck off!" Laughed the Bedford driver relishing a conversation that he had probably had several times before. "That's for the DS. You're in there." And he gleefully pointed to the left.

We looked to our left and saw some whitewashed stables that were, if memory serves, in an L shape.

We had a cold, cold week in that block. No heating and no running water apart from the river at the bottom of the hill that we were required do dunk ourselves into every morning. (See Adventure Training in volume 1 of We Were Cold Warriors for *that* exquisite torture.)

One day we were told we were going hiking with an overnight stop in tents that we were going to carry. As you are probably aware tents, poles, cookers, fuel, food, water, spare clothes etc for this kind of jaunt is not light. And in the army in 1981 'hiking' meant walking a *very* long way up and down *very* big hills carrying a *very* heavy pack. So once again we all climbed into the nice warm back of a bedford and were dropped off somewhere into shin deep snow. 99% of what we could see were made up of two colours. Blue sky and white snow. Look! A grey rock!

The instructors for this were not our sergeant instructors from Juniors, it was a couple of very tanned guys, one of whom had a South African accent. The rumour later on was that they were from a certain Regiment and were doing this for fun, but as you would expect this was never confirmed either way. I can tell you a few interesting things though. When we were trudging up a very steep hill something slid past me and made me jump. It was our tanned, odd-accented DS and he was sliding down the hill using his bergen as a sledge. To the groups absolute amazement he ran, yes RAN, up the hill and slid down two more times giggling like a toddler whilst we were trudging up it. We were completely unable to go any faster than we were going, which as I said, was a slow trudge, and he went up and down three times to our one. We looked at each other, saying nothing with our mouths, but our eyes said it all. And his bergen wasn't light either. Later on I had to move it and it weighed at least twice as much as mine.

Also, he was wearing a Walkman (Ah, the eighties) and didn't engage us in conversation at all. If we spoke to him with an inane comment (as you do when you are sixteen and trying to get on the right side of someone who can make your life difficult) he would smile in a friendly way, lift an earpiece and ask you to repeat. After you had said whatever nonsense you wanted to say he would cheerfully agree and plop it back on his ear. He wasn't being rude, he had just sensibly decided that there wasn't likely to be much of interest that a 16-year-old was going to say to him. It was at this point that I realised he was there to stop us dying, but not much more.

So this DS guy would pick one of our group and give him the six figure grid of where we were and a six figure grid of where he wanted to be and stand back and let him sort it out. But the DS would make sure he did it on his own without some smart arse who could navigate taking over and doing it all. When the navigator for that leg was ready he would tell the DS which way he thought we should go. The DS would cheerfully say, "Right, let's go then." and taking this as confirmation it was the right way, off we would all go. The group had been issued several sets of maps and compasses and as I had been an army cadet for years before joining up I made damn sure I got one. I was well used to navigating with a map and compass, so I always listened in from a distance and checked that the navigator for that leg was taking us the right way before we set off. After all, if he goes wrong, we all go wrong.

Before I describe the moment when I became an adult I suppose I first must define what I think an adult is. Legally, we have your 18th birthday, but of course this is just an arbitrary date chosen for use by the law. I personally think that the difference is this. If an adult has a problem they think "How can I solve this?" If a child has a problem they go to an adult and say, "I have a problem," and expects the adult to sort it for them.

Here is when it happened. He set someone up to navigate the next leg that ended up on top of a huge hill and said that on top of it was a mountain hut that we could rest at for an hour or so and cook up some grub, check our feet, and have a bit of a recharge. To say we were desperate for this stop was an understatement, we were absolutely bollocksed and really needed that rest. As usual I had checked my map, and I agreed with the guy navigating that bit. It was one of the easier legs actually, down a bit into a saddle, then up a really big hill and the hut was on top. Simple.

So down and then up, up, up we went. We got to the top. No hut, just huge rocks the size of houses. We looked at the DS. He was sitting on a rock looking at the scenery nodding along to the tune coming through his earphones. The navigator looked at us. We looked at him.
"Where's the fucking hut?" asked someone.
"Dunno." I said. "It should be here though."
"Where is it then?" asked another irritably.
"Ask him." said someone to the navigator, nodding towards the DS.
The navigator hesitantly approached and said, "There's no hut Staff."
The earpiece was lifted, and a raised eyebrow invited him to repeat himself.
"There's no hut Staff."
"Where is it then?" said DS and dropped his earpiece back into place.
"He's not going to fucking help us!" hissed someone angrily.
There then started an ill tempered debate on where the hut was. At times it almost came to blows, but finally the group split into two evenly sized groups. One group (including me) insisted that everything looked right. This WAS the right hill. The other group eventually won the argument with the simple question, 'Where the fuck is the fucking hut then you fucking twat?' I had no answer for this and neither did anyone else. All attempts to get help from the DS were met with polite disinterest.
After about fifteen minutes of angry debate we had to face the fact that we MUST be on the wrong hill and therefore looked for another likely candidate. There was another hill in front of us and slightly off to the right, but it didn't feel right. There was no way we could be that wrong. When I voiced my opinion on the subject I was offered a good kicking, which I declined. The argument had been won and lost. It's not here, so therefore it might be there, and that was the end of it.

The navigator approached the DS, gave this opinion and he immediately stood up and said, "Ok, let's go." To our childish eyes this looked like confirmation that it was the right plan. So relieved, but with nagging uncertainty, off we went.

When we got to this next hilltop it was obviously not the right place. It was smooth and featureless and from the peak you could see the whole crown of the hill. There was no way the hut could be here.

The DS removed his headphones and called us across. He invited us to look back at the hilltop we had been arguing on.

"See that rock on the left pointing up like a finger?"

"Yeeeaaahhhhh," we all said peering intently.

"See that upside down V shaped bit sticking up to the right of it?"

"Uuuaaarrrrgghhhh." we replied.

"That's the roof of the hut. At no point where you more than fifty metres from it. Had you spread out and searched you would have found it in minutes."

Silence greeted this. The kind of heavy silence that I have only ever experienced in the army.

"Ah well." he said cheerfully. "Let's carry on then! Who wants to navigate the next bit?"

Murdering him was a nonstarter, so navigate on we did. But it taught me that the only person you can really rely on, and I mean reeeeaalllyy rely on is you. February 1981 on a Welsh mountain the child left forever, and I became an adult. Mostly.

Jonno DP. Alanbrooke Troop, Roberts Battery. Junior Leaders Regiment. February 1981.

"A handful of soldiers is always better than a mouthful of arguments."
Georg C. Lichtenberg

The Hohne Chronicles part 1. Joining up.

1959. I remember well the start of my two years in the British Army. There it was, the dreaded telegram. 'Report to the Army recruiting depot in Liverpool to undergo a medical, you have been called up to do your two-year National Service.'
I knew it was coming and had tried hard to get out of it. I had been down to see a mate who had contacts with the Merchant Seamans Union, and he had attempted to get me on a ship before Her Majesty decided to grab me. Alas, I missed the telegram asking me to report to the Port of London to pick up a ship as I was enjoying the delights of a holiday fishing and wenching on the Broads.
In fact I could have missed the whole thing if it were not for my wenching days. You see, I had been deferred from the Army as I was doing an apprenticeship as an electrician. I had just completed my five-years and was being deferred again because I was doing a National Certificate in Electrical Engineering. It was a good deal. I was being paid to attend Carlett Park College to pass the necessary exams, but unfortunately while working as a sparky at the Ellesmere Port Cottage Hospital I fell madly in lust with this lovely blonde nursing cadet. I trotted her out for a few months and everything was hunky dory until she had move to Southport for further training. I started to skip classes and travel to Southport to see her, and to cut a long story short, I had my deferment cancelled. Bugger!
As instructed by the dreaded telegram I duly arrived at the army recruiting centre in Liverpool and the process began. Name, address, trade etc, (as if they didn't already know). I did all the tests, drop the tweeds, hand on my balls, cough. I must have coughed ok because the next thing said was, "FIT! What would you like to join?"

I said, "The Navy", but they didn't think this was funny and the Army Catering Corps was what the silly bastard came up with. I said, "I'm an electrician not a bloody cook", but he didn't take kindly to my helpful suggestion.

I suggested the Royal Engineers, then the REME, but he had his own idea, the Royal Signals. Well, I preferred it to the Catering Corps. This was the end of September 1959 and by November I had accepted my fate. One day I arrived home from work and a letter stamped O.H.M.S is on the mat. (Ironic considering I was an electrician trying to resist joining the army.) Inside was a postal order for half a crown, (about 30 pence), a travel warrant to Richmond in Yorkshire and two weeks notice of the end of my world.

I had started a late apprenticeship (17 ½) and had been deferred till I was caught (thanks again Sandra Ashcroft, wherever you are) at the ripe old age of twenty-two and a half. I was one of the oldest on the train heading for my two years of duty.

We arrived in Richmond about 3 o'clock in the afternoon, dressed in our best clobber, flare bottomed trousers, semi-drape suits and jackets, all the latest gear. We were all laughing, joking, and full of bravado, but then that thing happened which has been experienced by god knows how many people over god knows how many years. Out of nowhere these monsters emerged, the laughing stopped, and all hell broke loose. I don't know where they came from but there was a one stripe, two stripes and a sergeant. These maniacs in uniform had creases in their trousers you could cut paper with and with boots shining like the sun started screaming at us. They were telling us at the top of their amazingly loud voices to form up into groups.

"SIGNALS OVER HERE, TANKIES OVER THERE!", bawled one angry specimen, and after we had been separated we were ushered into the back of three-ton bedford trucks for the journey. Catterick was one of the biggest camps in Britain at the time, out in the wilds of Yorkshire with miles and miles of tank and artillery ranges, and it was going to be home for the next four weeks. Our unhappiness was enlivened by more polite requests when we arrived and the camp. "PICK UP THOSE FUCKING BAGS, GET FELL IN, TALLEST ON THE RIGHT, SHORTEST ON THE FUCKING LEFT!!!"

At five foot three inches I was always on the fucking left. "COME ON, MOVE!!! YOU'RE NOT AT HOME WITH MUMMY NOW, YOU BELONG TO ME!! The abuse just kept coming like hailstones, it had to be experienced to be believed. We didn't know what had hit us, they yelled and screamed constantly, but what they were attempting to achieve was hard to work out. We, the Royal Signals personnel, were to do our basic training at 26 Signals Regiment and we were marched off to some Nissan huts in the vast camp. I say marched, it was more of a shuffle really. We lined up outside a hut waiting for our chance to be turned into solders of the Queen. Inside were dozens of tables with an officer or NCO seated at each one, and from going in to coming out our lives were completely changed. By the time we exited that building the army owned us, lock, stock and well-oiled barrel. This induction process started with the usual interrogation, and I filled in form after form after form until I was allocated my new identity: 23755279 Signalman Travers JB and don't you forget it. It only took a couple of days to remember the number and like everyone else I will remember that number until I shuffle off this mortal coil. For the first few days you had to recite your number every time you addressed an NCO or officer, and lookout if you forgot it. After we had filled in all the forms we were lined up outside and marched to the QM stores for kitting out. Nothing fitted us to say the least, especially for me. I was so small (5 ft 3 ½ inches), I think that I was the smallest you could be to be in the Army. I also only weighed 7 stone. We were issued all of our kit (I say issued, it was hurled at us at lightning speed, four blankets, two sheets, pillows and pillowcases, knife, fork and spoon, mug –white, porcelain, drinking for the use of, three hairy shirts khaki, two pairs of trousers khaki, one belt and one tin of blanco to keep it clean, two battledresses, underwear, three pairs woollen socks khaki, one greatcoat (bloody cold at Christmas in Catterick I can tell you), one housewife (needle, cotton, and darning equipment), you name it we got it, and as I said before, nothing fitted. Using the greatcoat was like putting on a marquee and it all stank of mothballs.

I got to the boots section and the bastard behind the counter screams at me, "SIZE?!"

I screamed back, "SIZE FIVE SERGEANT!"

He returned, "NO ONE TAKES A FUCKING SIZE FIVE, YOU A FUCKING MIDGET OR SOMETHING?!"

He issued me with a six. I put my foot in it, laced it up, and rattled my foot around. It took a lot of convincing that sixes were far too big, and finally he relented. The mean bastard, you would think he was paying for them. After various insults, mockery etc, he issued me with one pair of 'Boots Officers, hiking, for the use of' and one pair of 'Boots Officers, climbing, for the use of'. Apparently only officers have size five feet. Both pairs are very different from everyone else's, which is not great in basic training. One pair had sets of studs set in groups of three and the other pair had cleats, one of which was in the middle of the instep. The biggest difference was the fact they were brown, yes bloody brown.

Bastards!

By now it's getting very late, and we have not been fed since we got off the train, and a lot of these boys had never been away from their mums before and were scared witless by what had happened. Fortunately for me I had worked around the country on various construction contracts and was used to being away from home, but still, I hadn't expected anything like this, and I felt sorry for a lot of these guys.

After we had been kitted out they marched us off to our barrack blocks which were two storied buildings and we were allocated a room with twelve beds in it. We each picked a bed and dumped our pile of kit on it, before being marched off to the mess hall for a meal, shiny new KFS and mug in hand. It was a pretty basic meal of warmed up leftovers from the regiment's teatime and after having lived a life of pampering from mothers it was one hell of a shock to the system for a lot of the recruits. After that it was into a lecture room, and we were told that by morning we were expected to have our gear pressed, boots polished and be ready for inspection. Reveille is at 6am, Breakfast is at 7am and the first parade is at 8am, the parade ground is right outside the barracks. It was now about midnight and we are expected to make our beds, so we can get some sleep.

First though, we are shown how to present our gear every morning before going on parade. We have four blankets and two sheets. The first blanket is folded and laid out making a long strip and the second blanket is carefully folded and is placed on top of it. Then a sheet, then another blanket, then the second sheet then the last blanket. Around this stack the first blanket was wrapped making a very tidy right-angled rectangle of bedding. That was the intention anyway. Woe betide you if any of the sheets or blankets were out of line, or it didn't make a solid tidy pack. The inspecting officer/NCO would just pick it up and toss it out of the upstairs window into the garden below. No kidding. Off you would trot and pick it up and try again.

By the time this was demonstrated it was well after midnight and we still had our uniforms to press and our boots to polish before we can get some sleep. And I have another problem. My boots are brown, and they should be black like everyone else's. However, theirs all have pimples on them and they must be removed over the next few days by heating a spoon over a candle and then pressing on the pimples to soften them and rub until smooth.

As I said, I didn't have that problem, but they still had to be dyed black and polished by morning. The QM had issued me with a couple of bottles of black clothes dye so my first job was to dye them black before I could start to shine them. I must admit though, the drill cadre did give me a bit of leeway for the first couple of days.

My barrack room was right next to the drill instructors' room (two of them, both Corporals) so they had this system to help us remember our army numbers. In their room was a radiator and every time they rattled a tin mug or drill stick along it you could hear it in our room. One of the signalmen from the room had to rush into their barrack room, stand to attention and recite their name, rank and serial number.

"23755279 Signalman Travers JB, permission to speak Corporal?"

"Yes Signalman, what is it?"

"You rang, Corporal."

"Oh yes, go and run me a shower (or any other little chore they needed doing), dismissed."

We soon learned our numbers, while most of the other rooms struggled for a few days.

We also had to do cookhouse fatigues, mooloo parades (picking up rubbish) and anything else the army decided we needed to do to be kept busy and on our toes. All this for ten shillings and sixpence a week, but after four weeks it went up to a pound. Out of that grand sum they took sixpence for barrack room damages whether something got broken or not and sixpence for haircuts whether you needed one or not.

L/Cpl J.B. Travers. 207 Signals Squadron. 7th Armoured Brigade 1960/61.

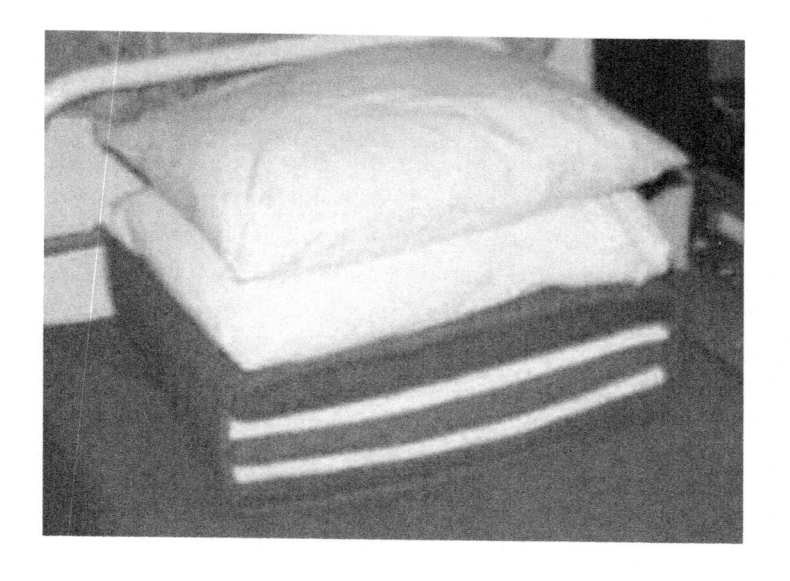

The bed block. Possibly the most pointless thing you ever did.

A damp dry day

If you have never been in the Royal Artillery you will not know that the majority of time on exercise you are 'dry' firing. In other words you are out in the field doing everything you would do in war (cam nets, laying the gun, getting rained on) but not actually firing any whizzbangnastys out of the barrel. What's more, most artillery firing is indirect, which means the crew can't see the target, but its position relative to the distant target is calculated mathematically and the command post tells you to aim on a certain bearing and elevation. This means anyone seeking an exciting day out watching an artillery gun dry firing will find it distinctly dull. It will be a group of soldiers standing around a gun smoking and swearing whilst occasional minute changes are made to the aim. For hours and hours and hours.
I was in 32 regiment Royal Artillery in the sixties and my gun sub was told to deploy into a waterlogged field and set up for dry firing. Oh the irony. This makes it sound leisurely, but when a British artillery unit comes into action it is anything but. Our equipment was a lorry called a Mac and an 8-inch howitzer. I don't know what the combined weight is but it's quite a lot so we started persuading 2nd Lieutenant Muirhead, or 2nd Lieutenant Pinhead as we called him, that we thought it probable we would get bogged in in that field and that would upset the BC, who he was terrified of.
He looked worried.
"Also, it might get damaged." chipped in someone else.
"We would be less likely to get bogged in if we stayed close to that barn." surmised another.
In reality it was chucking down and we were just trying it on, as you do. Nowadays lots of artillery is self-propelled (looks like a tank) so you can shut the hatches and stay dry, but the 8-inch

howitzer was not, it was basically a gun barrel on wheels and if it rained you got wet, if it rained a lot you got very wet.

Pinhead was a gentle sort who, rumour had it, been made to join the army by his dad as it was a family tradition and unusually for an officer was quite easy to persuade.

So the day started.

"FIRE MISSION BATTERY!!" Came over the net and the required response was sent by us.

The CP sent us (and the rest of the battery) fire missions all morning, and they got the required message back from us each time, and it was all going swimmingly until the Battery Commander turned up banging on the door.

This is when he discovered we were not in the muddy field, we were in fact in the dry barn. Not only were *we* in the dry barn, so was the gun, which we hadn't even bothered unhitching off the back of the Mac. We were sat around heroically drinking tea, smoking and playing cards whilst one of us was answering the CP on the net. What hadn't improved his temper was wandering around in the rain before he decided to check the barn.

To say the BC was upset is an understatement. He absolutely did his fucking nut, Pinhead shat himself and we were trying not to laugh.

Chinney. 32 Regiment Royal Artillery.

"If you want to go fast, go alone. If you want to go far, go with friends"
Anon

My Adjutant was not a nice man

After I finished basic training I was posted to my infantry battalion that was stationed near Salisbury and as you would expect we had a lot of PT in our schedule. Captain David Fladgate was the adjutant and he was a complete martinet who was always looking for trouble and never passed up an opportunity to show off how clever or tough he was. But one day he came unstuck...

He decided one morning that HQ Platoon needed some fresh air and exercise. Ok, off we went on the road from Knook to Chitterne in Somerset. After a bit he stopped and told us to go into a nearby field and pair off. Once we had done this he told us to face each other, grab hold of each other's shoulders and on the word of command – push and try to get the other guy on the floor. Now I was lucky in a way, because before I joined up I had been an apprentice builder and a keen cyclist so I was extremely fit. In fact I found my basic training to be a piece of cake really compared to some of the lads. Anyway, we started doing this wrestling and I quickly put the lad down. Captain Fladgate stopped the platoon told us to swap partners with someone else and do it again. "Ok," he said, "again, on the word of command, push." Within seconds I had the second lad down as well.

Captain Fladgate decided this was an opportunity for him to demonstrate to the rest of the platoon how tough he was. So he walked over, squared up to me, and said, "So you think you're tough do you?" I hadn't been in the army long, but I'd been in long enough to know there was no correct answer to that question. So I said nothing. "Ok." he said, glaring at me, "When I say push try and get me on the floor".

It probably wasn't the cleverest decision I've ever made but I decided not to let him win just to keep him happy. When he

said 'push' I had him on the floor even faster than the other two guys. At least he had enough sense to not have another go and I mostly succeeded in keeping a grin off my face.
"Right!" He said, picking himself up and brushing bits of grass off. "Let's carry on the exercise! On my command I want you to run backwards up that hill! GO!"
It was obvious to everyone that it was revenge, and that he was trying to get the rest of the platoon to blame me, but to their credit they never did.
I was feeling quite happy when we jogged back to camp and several of the platoon said they would stand me a drink for making Fladgate look a fool, but of course you can't really win for long against someone like that.
It came back to haunt me a few weeks later when I was on guard duty. Off I went with everyone else to the guardroom ready for us to take over the guarding of the camp at six o'clock in the evening. I had got stick man the last two times I had guard duty, so I was quietly hoping to make it three in a row and had made sure my turnout was faultless. (If you don't know the army will mount one man more than they need for guard duty and the best turned out person gets 'stick man' and doesn't have to do the guard duty.) As usual we were inspected by the guard commander and the orderly sergeant and were standing at ease outside the guardroom awaiting the arrival of the orderly officer. With my eyes firmly to the front I heard him approach and we were called to attention.
'In the bag.' I thought confidently.
As usual the Orderly Officer started at one end and worked his way down the line until he got to me.
It was Fladgate.
I did not get stick man.
I did not get the night off.
But I did get jailed on the spot for being idle on parade. (Seriously, they even wrote it on the board.) I got my

permanent pass cancelled (the one that allows you to leave camp in civvies in the evening), and I got several days on jankers. Fun times!

Private John Case, HQ Company, 1st Wiltshire Regiment. 1954 – 1956.

Interesting military stuff #1. Weird Pistol facts.

You may be surprised to learn that Britain's RAF and Fleet Air Arm pilots use a German World War II pistol as their personal protection. It's the Walther PP which is the slightly larger version of the Walther PPK that James Bond uses and it entered service with the German army in 1935. It's a blowback operated semi-automatic and as you would expect from the Germans extremely well made. British military liking for this pistol started in 1974 when they bought 3000 of them, rechambered them to .22 to and issued them to the Ulster Defence Regiment for personal protection whilst off duty.

This compares with another odd World War II Allied/German pistol story. The allies used the Browning 9mm throughout the Second World War, mostly manufactured in Canada, and the British continued its use for many decades after that. During WWII the weapon was a favourite of the Special Air Service before being issued to all British military units.

The pistol was actually designed by an American called Browning and as well as being made in Canada it was manufactured from 1935 by a company called Fabrique Nationale in Belgium with the intention of selling it to the French army. Obviously that business idea fell through as there wasn't a French army to sell it to after 1940. (Fabrique Nationale are the same people who designed the SLR rifle by the way.)

When the factory was captured early on in World War II the Germans were impressed with the pistol and had them continue the manufacture of it, issuing it to several units including German paratroopers and the SS.

An incredible thought isn't it? During WWII the SAS and the SS used the same pistol!

The Browning pistol continued to be widely manufactured and production only ceased in 2018 except for a few small places around the world that still manufacture it under licence. Several countries still use this weapon, even the Belgians!

Researched and written by Jonno DP

Just keeping an eye on her

We were on exercise, parked up in some German wood somewhere. Nine Bedfords forming the Comcen plus Radio Delay... ahem... Radio Relay wagons, cookhouse wagon, REME wagon etc. A small footprint we did not have. As was standard in those days, the khazi was an upturned tea chest with a loo seat screwed to it over a hole dug by whoever had pissed of the SSM. The only head nod to modesty was a shoulder height (when seated) hessian screen.

One day, we discovered that we were getting a new Rodney posted in straight from the farm. Not only a Rodney but a female Rodney (a Rodette?). This was a first for our Squadron, in fact, I think for the Regiment. Anyway, we weren't savages, a fresh pit was dug, a new tea chest procured and we even found some flowery comfy bum loo paper. When she arrived, and as part of her tour, her personal khazi was pointed out to her. Three days went by and she still hadn't been. We knew this as a 'Ma'am watch' had been mounted (What?! Don't judge! Different times!). Eventually she succumbed to the basest of natures calls and the shout went out over the intercom, "She's off lads!"

As if by magic we were transformed into a mob of meerkats. Peeking out from everywhere. Perverts I hear you cry? Wait for it.

Just as she had her keks around knee height, bum heading towards the comfiest loo seat the SQMS could find, a voice from the depths of the pit was heard to cry, "Not yet Ma'am! I'm still fucking digging!" We (the Techs) had run a wire to a speaker screwed to the inside of the tea chest with a mic on

our end! Her poor head shot up above the hessian with such a look on her face!
Rodneys... gotta love 'em!

Frank McGoldrick, Royal Signals

What a prick

Several of us, especially me, were not very popular with the Battery Commander after a block inspection. Someone returning from a merry night out a brought back a fucking great cactus in a pot that they had nicked out of somebody's garden. We had set up some shelves on the wall by jamming them between two big radiator pipes and put the cactus and some books on it. It sounds dodgy, but it was alright as long as you were careful with it. Lieutenant Pinhead and the BC had come in and we're doing the usual officer burble that they do during inspections. The BC didn't like the look of our jerry built shelves and gave them a tug. The shelf immediately fell off the wall, the cactus bounced on the floor and embedded itself spikes first in the back of Pinheads legs. He started hopping around the room screaming in pain and we failed completely to not laugh. It really was a 'Welease Woger' moment and we were all laughing, it was impossible not to. His dignity suffered another blow when we walked past one of the single rooms after the inspection and we saw him sitting on someone's bed with his trousers around his ankles pulling the spikes out one by one. In the end the BC got so fed up with me he posted me to Woolwich depot. But as punishments go it was a failure, I had a great time there. I never owned a car whilst I was there, but I always had an army one to drive around in, fuelled by army petrol of course, and when I got out after my six years I may have had only 90 quid to my name but my house was fully furnished. Mind you most of the furniture had crows feet stamped on it.

The army didn't pay much in those days so alternative methods had to be found to supplement your income. One time we were in a camp near Okehampton and I wanted to go out on the piss but I didn't have any money, so a quick trip to the cookhouse and I was off with a twenty five pound box of frozen haddock that I carried into town and tried hawking around a few hotels, but they all fucked me off. Eventually I unloaded it at the local fish and chip shop for a fiver (which was plenty enough to get pissed on in those days), but the best money maker I ever had was when they were stupid enough to let me run the disco in Woolwich. In those days civilians were allowed in and any money made was to be donated to the PRI. Well, the PRI didn't see much of it, but I was always flush. Decades later I bumped into my mate who did the scam with me and was amazed to find he was the CEO of a HUGE American company. We chatted for a bit and then I asked, "How the fuck did you end up as a CEO of a company?" He gave me a sly smile and said, "It takes a thief to know a thief."

Chinney. 32 Regiment Royal Artillery.

The Hohne Chronicles part 2. Basic training.

After a briefing from our platoon officer, we were ushered into a lecture theatre where we were given a brief introduction to our fate for the initial four weeks of basic training. Firstly, we had to go back to our barracks and parcel up all our civilian clothes and post them home. We were, as they say, In The Army Now.
For the next four weeks right up until Christmas eve, it was rifle drill, marching drill, PT, jankers, (cookhouse fatigues, I must say I loved peeling spuds, yuck!) indoctrination, smoke breaks, bulling boots, pressing uniforms, and twice a day we were marched to the NAAFI for a ten-minute break, that is a bun and a mug of tea. You can't get much on nine and sixpence a week, but then, there wasn't much worth having. After about three weeks we had trade selection boards to attend.
I remember mine like yesterday, it was classic army. Outside the room was a blackboard with a load of trades for us to select. Being an electrician, I chose 'Electrician'. This jumped-up Captain glared at me. "What did you do in civvy street?"
"I was an electrician, Sir."
"Sorry pick something else".
I picked Linesman.
"No pick again."
To speed up the rejections and save time I turned to face him. "Despatch rider Sir?"
His lip curled, "Have you ever ridden a motor bike, Signalman?" he sneered.
"Yes Sir," I said patiently, "I have one at home".
"No pick again, come on hurry up we have others waiting."
I looked back at my dwindling options on the board.
"Hold up your hands and wriggle your fingers." said the captain impatiently.

Mystified, I complied. "Right!" says he, "Teleprinter operator/signal centre operator! Next!"
And that was it for the next two years. What bullshit that turned out to be. Maybe I should have gone into the catering corps after all. Just joking.
In fact, it was probably one of the best things that happened because I have used my typing skills to great advantage ever since, especially with the advent of modern technology.
My first day in the gym was quite an experience. There we were, about forty guys of all shapes and sizes all lined up and the PTI, 51% muscle and 49%, ego walks along the line. He selected the fat guy, the skinny guys and me, and tells us to move to one side. What was left was a bunch of brawny, fit, nasty looking bastards. He explains that we must pass a series of tests over the next four weeks and if we fail, we will be sent to the fitness centre at the signals depot in York until we could pass said tests. This was not a tempting prospect; basic training was bad enough.
The tests consisted of ten heaves to the beam, ten shins to the beam and ten press ups. The reason for his selecting us was that he suspected we couldn't do it, but he would give us the chance after the gorillas had done theirs. It was surprising how many of the athletic looking fellas could not make it, and how many of the selected invalids passed first time.
When it was my turn he screamed, "TEN HEAVES TO THE BEAM SIGNALMAN, GO!!" and turned back to the squad.
Well with my body weight to muscle ratio, it was no problem for me at all and I did it really quick. When he turned back to me I had finished and was just hanging there. Thinking I was being lazy he angrily screamed, "TEN HEAVES TO THE BEAM!!" Well, I did another ten and the same thing happened, he turned away and didn't see it. As I was hanging there it was starting to hurt and I gave a small whimper. "DON'T FUCKING ARGUE SOLDIER, GET ON WITH IT!!"

After another ten (so that's thirty heaves to the beam) I was really starting to struggle but he just told me to get back into the squad and that was it, I had passed! The guys who couldn't manage it were given the next four weeks to pass the tests, and only two never made the grade and ended up in York. Much to my relief it was the last time I was singled out for any reason, I was no longer regarded as the runt of the litter you might say. I was classed as P3. The Army assessed everyone with a system called PULHHEEMS, this categorised your ability to perform your duties, P was physique, U Upper limbs, L Lower limbs, Hearing right, Hearing left, Eyesight right, Eyesight Left, Mental function and Stability. P3 was physique 'slight', which meant no marching over a mile. Great! I thought until I found out the alternative. If the squad had a five-mile hike or a ten-mile hike, I could either volunteer to do it, or spend the day in the cookhouse washing dishes and peeling spuds, starting at 5.30 in the morning.

"No thanks," I would say, "I'll do the march."

"Very sporting of you Signalman," they would remark.

"Sporting my arse." was my silent thought, but the next four weeks were among the toughest of my life.

L/Cpl J.B. Travers. 207 Signals Squadron. 7th Armoured Brigade 1960/61.

Signalman Travers JB. 3rd from left second row.
Pass out Photo.

In 1944 at the battle of Arnhem the 16,000 German troops surrounding the 740 British troops sent a message to the British Commander to discuss surrender. He replied "Sorry, we don't have the facilities to take you all prisoner."

A Not So Merry Christmas

This is a story that may sail a little too close to the rules of the Official Secrets Act so I'll keep quiet about the location as the facilities are still there, even though it's 50 years since this story took place and it's probably available for anyone to study on Google maps.

So anyway, it all starts in Hohnelager where I was stationed from 1967 to 1970 with the 2nd Royal Tank Regiment. It was a huge garrison town consisting of barracks, married quarters and vehicle hangars for NATO forces, all left over from the war. When it came to Christmas duties the married men were usually allowed to stay at home with their families while us single guys had to pick up the slack with guards etc so for the three years I was there, I only spent one Christmas in the camp. That one year was spent in something of a drunken haze, so I don't remember which year or what I did.

The other two years was spent guarding a nuclear weapon site some two hundred kilometres to the south. Why *our* regiment had to carry out this duty at Christmas two years running, only personnel of a higher rank than mine would know. Perhaps our CO volunteered us using that well known phrase taught during officer training, 'My men would be happy to serve'. As if. Typically, there were perhaps twenty of us sent on this site guard, and while the officer embarked in a heated and draught free land rover, us oiks piled into the back of an army truck with a canvas top, with the temperature hovering around zero. For some reason I can't remember, we also took with us a Mark 1 ferret scout car. To the uninitiated this is an armoured car, and the Mark 1 is distinctive because it doesn't have a turret. The driver doesn't have a windscreen and observes the road through three hatches, one to each side and another in the front. The air filters for the engine are actually *inside* the vehicle, so even stationary its draughty, and as soon as you move you are blasted with air. Imagine driving an open topped car with no windscreen in winter and you have it.

A ferret mark 1. Fucking thing.

It's even worse for the poor guy commanding the vehicle. Since the drivers' view is severely restricted, the commander sits in the open turret and takes responsibility for ensuring that the driver is pointing in the right direction. But he gets a double-whammy; the indirect ram-air effect coming through the drivers' hatches, cooling his lower body, plus the direct effect of wind, rain, sleet and snow cooling his upper body. Lovely. But more of this later.
So we have a couple of trucks, a land rover and a ferret driving in convoy, which by some unwritten rule, travels about 20 mph and rarely goes any faster. The wind is whipping through the gaps in the canvas, it's freezing cold and we have to put up with

this for a couple of hours. When we arrive at the barracks for the first night we are cold and miserable except for the officer who has just enjoyed a leisurely drive through the German countryside. Our reward for this travail was a bare room, beds with mattresses but no blankets, and a night cocooned in an army issue sleeping bag thin enough to see through.

The next day we were issued with live ammunition for our sterling sub-machine guns but were told to tape the magazines up just in case anyone tried to shoot someone, and then travelled the short distance to the site we were to guard. It was made up of three separate compounds, all enclosed in high, barbed wire fences with guard towers like the prison camp in The Great Escape. The guard towers surround the inner compound where the nuclear warheads were kept and was guarded by the Americans. They got a lot of verbal flak from the Brits, because uncharacteristically, they seemed to be a surly uncommunicative lot. The other two smaller compounds comprised of the missile hangars, and another for the rocket motors which us Brits guarded.

We had two brick-built accommodation blocks, one for each compound. Once again, it was beds with bare mattresses and sleeping bags, but at least it was warm inside. Outside it was a different matter, something like a foot of snow, and temperatures well below zero. Now someone once said that warfare was 99% boredom, followed by 1% sheer terror. Well, I can assure anyone who hasn't experienced it that guard duty (of any kind) is 100% boredom. I can't remember the shift pattern, but it was something like four hours on, four hours QRF, four hours off. We read books, slept, and played board games for the 'off' hours, while the 'on' hours were spent huddled in a sentry box, trying to keep warm and awake.

One year, I was on duty as second in command of the rocket motor compound, which was connected to the missile compound by an old WW2 field telephone. You've seen the movies, wind it up and talk. With a bit of luck you can just about hear what is being said by the bloke at the other end. I'm nominally in charge as the guy in command is asleep when the telephone rings and I get an indistinct message which went something like, 'Wake up the QRF *crackle.. fizz..* check the perimeter.. *crackle... click...* two men...*click... fizz... fart noise...* loaded magazines', which I took to mean, "Wake up the guard, fit loaded magazines and search the perimeter for two men acting suspiciously."

As I've often said, I was a stupid soldier, so instead of checking that I had heard correctly, I woke the QRF and told them to gallop off in search of the intruder. I was in the process of taking the tape off my magazine when the guard commander, who had more gumption than I did, phoned back to confirm the order. It transpired that through a combination of a bad telephone line and said stupidity, I had misheard the message. What was really said, was to 'Wake the QRF and get them to search for two loaded magazines which had gone missing!' That misunderstanding could have got me into lots of bother, which would have happened had not the loss of loaded magazines been a more serious offence.

Guard duty carried on for a week over Christmas and New Year. Boring, boring, boring. No Soviet aggression, no terrorist attacks, nothing exciting or even slightly interesting for seven days. The only highlight was at the end, and I can only guess that counting and returning live ammo was more hassle than it was worth, so we fired it off! No, not in the air like an Arab wedding party, but on the local 25 metre shooting range where we got to finally take the tape off our magazines. It was still freezing cold and it must have been an unofficial arrangement because everyone got a No.12 target which was about two feet by two feet – except me. I got a target normally used for pistol shooting at ten metres, which was only twelve inches by six inches. At 25 metres it was just a dot in the distance.

However, what followed was the best shooting I did in my whole army career. I had fired off about twenty rounds when I had a misfire, that is, I pulled the trigger, but got only a click from the weapon and nothing else. I kept the gun pointing down the range and raised my arm to call over the range commander. The rules are very strict about this, range commanders get very upset if you wave a loaded weapon in his face whilst telling them, "It doesn't work!" and is usually followed by a bellowed command to, "Get off my bloody range", or worse. Anyway, I cocked the weapon which ejected the dodgy round and carried on firing. When I inspected the target a short while later, I had twenty-nine hits from twenty-nine rounds fired!

The final incident happened on the journey home. The ferret scout car was sick, very sick, and would barely start and for some reason they needed a different commander, (remember, the guy who would sit with his upper body in the wind and weather whilst his lower body was air cooled). They asked for volunteers and in true Army style it was decided that I was the volunteer. Oh goody.

I spent the next six hours driving at 20mph trying to avoid frost bite.

It is said that wind-chill equates to something like 1°C for every 1mph. The weather forecast said the air temperature was -6°C, so travelling at 20mph, I estimate that my personal air temperature was about minus 26°C. I wiggled my toes, flapped my arms, but it was no good; it still felt colder than a modern freezer (which is about minus 18°C if you are interested). We couldn't stop for a warm drink in case the engine wouldn't start again, so we just trundled along until we finally arrived back at camp. I ordered the driver to park outside the NAAFI and said after I got out he was to drive the ferret back to the hangar. I was so cold I could hardly move, so I sort of rolled out of the bloody thing and staggered into the bar. One double rum didn't help, but two or three more, got the blood flowing a bit. I've been cold before, and I've been cold since, but I've never felt so cold as that.

So there we go. Christmas in a tank regiment. No tinsel. No carols, and definitely no festive cheer.

Gordon Simmonds 2RTR

"In the midst of chaos, there is also opportunity"
Sun Tzu, The Art of War. (And a gunner who's name I forget watching the QM's stores catch fire.)

Hard targeting

While at 22 Signal Regiment, I took up Judo and ended up helping with the garrisons kids club. One of the other judokas (got a be one to understand) was from our neighbour regiment 27 (or maybe 49) Field Regiment RA. They were in the middle of their pre-deployment training for NI, buggering about practicing VCPs and generally disturbing everyone's day.
After judo club one night and a few beers in the NAAFI bar my RA mate and me headed downtown. We were both a bit skint so shanksies pony was the form of transport. Soon the baseball bat of fresh air on top of drunkenness had hit us both squarely between the eyes and we decided it was a good idea to practice hard targeting on our way to town. Dashing down alleys, crouching in doorways. All the best moves from those press images of Belfast. Whilst he was halfway across the road a car comes along and catches my oppo in its headlights. Of course, he pulls his invisible 9mm pistol and draws a bead on the driver, who calmly reaches over and flicks on the blue lights... Uh oh! ... Die Polizei! My oppo did the best thing he could... cleared his invisible 9mm, laid it on the ground and laid down beside it, hands behind his head. From my hiding place, (oppo goes only so far in this movie!), I saw the pair of coppers disembark from the vehicle, do that thing where they flick open the holsters in case they need to get their pistols out quick, (German coppers carry pistols if you didn't know), and walk up to my oppo. They spend some time looking for the invisible 9mm but... being invisible they couldn't find it. They muttered something along the lines of "Verdamt Englishe soldate," told him to get up, shook their heads and climbed back in their car heading to the next interaction of the night, no doubt with another pissed up squaddie!

Frank McGoldrick, Royal Signals

Fun lovin' criminals

I had some good laughs serving in the Artillery. After a night on the lash the lads had been nicking a few too many bicycles for the locals taste and complaints had been made. These complaints worked their way down to the RSM who got himself worked up in to a right old RSM style rage over it. He ordered that the regiment be paraded on the square later that day so he could do his thing. We all dutifully formed up, marched over to the square and after the usual warnings we waited for The Man to arrive. After a bit he did and started in the expected way.
"I AM DISGUSTED AT THE BEHAVIOUR OF SOLDIERS IN THIS REGIMENT…….. GOOD RELATIONSHIPS WITH THE LOCALS……. NO ONE LIKES A THIEF…… JUST AS GUILTY IF YOU USE A STOLEN BIKE….. QUEENS REGS…. DISCIPLINE… STANDARDS.. etc.
He got steadily angrier with us though, because he kept seeing people trying not to laugh and threats of jail abounded. Why were we struggling to not be amused? Well, his office was a long way from the square and he had either borrowed, or being an RSM 'borrowed' someones bicycle to make the journey. Yes, you guessed it. It was one we had nicked last night…

Gunner 'X' Royal Artillery

That's why they are called thunderboxes

After a rather arduous battle-camp (Signals practising our infantry skills) in Vogelsang, we gathered ready for endex to be given. The OC was a guy called Gary 'Digger' Barnes, an Australian Exchange Officer and ex Australian SAS. He had a good sense of humour and was very popular with the lads but on this particular day it went a bit too far. I saw him going into a portaloo and asked, "Who's got a thunderflash?"
I'm not sure who actually had it nor who dropped it into the vent tube but there was a dull THWUMP!! and about 100 litres of shit sludged up and down the inside of the portaloo. It was quite visible as the light blue plastic turned dark. It was exactly as I had expected, but as I said, not actually done by me. Unfortunately, Digger had heard my voice asking about the thunderflash, so I was the only thought in the mind of an ex SAS bloke covered in shit who was not happy in the slightest. He bolted out of the thunderbox and made a beeline for me. I didn't actually click what was happening until I could see the whites of his eyes (like snow-holes in the shit), staring at me like a man possessed. Nobody stopped him, and as he was covered in it no one wanted to, besides they were pissing themselves laughing. So I took the beating that was due to me for having the idea and afterwards we were hosed down together and given soap and disinfectant. I wasn't too happy, as I had already changed into clean combats, so had to put my stinking exercise ones back on. Neither of us kept the shit-soaked ones, they were binned. He didn't hold any grudges though. A month or so later I had to come back from summer

camp early and he gave me a lift in his Porsche 911 and even let me drive it for a couple of hundred miles.

Gaz Duffy, Royal Signals (1985-2010)

Dogs and the depot

HQ 3 Base Ammunition Depot (3 BAD) was established in 1946 and by the mid-1980s was the largest Ammunition Depot in Western Europe covering around 1300 Hectares, which is about 1,800 football pitches or eleven and a half square kilometres. We had dog patrols during silent hours, and weekends doing a four-hour patrol around the depot then four off. A few of the dog handlers were Brits or Dutch that could speak good English, but most of them were German or Turkish. Of course, being an ammo depot certain items were strictly controlled. Cigarettes, food and drink for example were not allowed in and as depot security it was our job to fill in patrol sheets at the guard room when the dog patrols phoned in from the hundreds of fire phones around the depot. We also had mobile security fence patrols that went around in land rovers and in winter there was a really odd coincidence that kept occurring.

Amazingly, when doing the mobile patrol, we would regularly happen to bump into the Brit and Dutch dog handlers at one of the Sangers dotted about the fence line and entrances. Lots of the brits were ex forces, who had married German women and stayed in Germany.

So we'd end up in a Sanger with the dog handler and his dog, out came the guards sandwiches, a flask of coffee and the smokes. After this we would all get in the vehicle and drop the dog handler at his next phone-in point. If it was really cold we'd take him to the next point as well. After dropping him off we would go and find the next Brit dog handler. I'm sure they appreciated the hot coffee, sandwich and smoke.

Spike Elliott MT/MHE Bracht 1987-1990

Myths and Legends. Stephen 'Goat' Harris, AKA Liquid Len

When I was in the army I knew a guy called Goat Harris, (also known as Liquid Len), who was, was to put it bluntly, very odd! I suppose to cover myself for legal reasons all of the following did happen, but my understanding is that now he is a respectable husband and father!
I arrived in Warminster in late 1979 and Goat, who was working as an SQMS store man, welcomed me. He was pretty drunk as he was celebrating his birthday and I endured what can only be described as a nightmare of an evening drinking with him.
The following morning, very much the worse for wear, I went to the washroom to wash and shave before a days work on the tank park. The washroom was big enough to accommodate fourteen soldiers conducting morning ablutions, but I was forced to join a queue snaking out into the corridor. Unfortunately for us, there was only one sink that could be used as the remainder contained bits of a motor bike engine that belonged to Goat. The motor bike frame was propped up in a shower and various tools and bits of bike were everywhere. Eventually, the motor bike was restored and he often gave me and others a lift to Westbury railway station to catch the train home on a Friday afternoon. In those days, there was a ramp that you had to walk up to get onto the platforms, and many a time Goat risked the wrath of the Station Master and the many train spotters that were on the platform as he raced up the ramp on the bike, the engine reverberating loudly as it passed through the tunnel under Platform one. He would roar along the platform and drop me off alongside the carriage of my choice still dressed in black overalls, having been on the tank park only some thirty minutes previously.

On one occasion, Goat took his motor bike on the train and prior to the change of trains at Exeter for the onward journey to Plymouth he started it up. A frantic guard came running in and attempted to get him to turn it off, but Goat just acted deaf and mute and filled the carriage up with fumes!

Goat was quite content to do guard duties for people providing the money was right. Whilst on guard Goat would use the Duty Vehicle (a one tonne Land Rover) to drop people of at various locations for an evenings drinking and then would return at an agreed time to pick them up and return them to camp.

One evening Bob Kessell and myself were on the pull and Goat gave us a lift to a small village near Warminster where there was a disco of some description in the Village Hall. Bob spent a few minutes on the dance floor, most of which was spent walking around on his hands, and then copped off with some bird. I, meanwhile, had decided that I was going to give the Vicar's wife a good sorting as she looked up for it! Chewing on a cucumber sandwich from the buffet, I promised that I would help in any way I could to help raise funds for the church roof. She was delighted and spent some time explaining to her husband what a fine chap I was. Oh, if only she knew!

After one or two dances and sadly realising that the Vicars wife was going to keep her pants on, it was time to go back to camp, so we rang the Guard Room and asked Goat to come and get us. Well actually it was just me, as Bob had gone home with the bird who had been so impressed with his hand walking. Goat pulled up into the car park and realising that he needed to turn around, he drove onto an adjacent field and spun the rover around using a handbrake turn. I heard somebody shout the words, "He has hit the cricket wicket". Oh bollocks!

A smiling Goat stopped and I jumped in and told him to put his foot down quick! Leaving the car park with spinning wheels showering people with gravel we headed towards Warminster and after a few minutes we saw Bob Kessell running towards us in the middle of the road frantically waving his arms. Goat stopped, Bob jumped into the back and for the second time Goat revved the engine and wheel span us on our way. A shout of, "I will get you, you twaatttt...." could be heard from behind us as we accelerated up the A36 towards Warminster.

Apparently, Bob and his new lady friend had been in a caravan in the back of her garden discussing philosophy and sipping tea with his trousers around his ankles when the girls father noticed the rocking motion of said caravan. His intervention had persuaded Bob that the evening was over.

On the odd occasion Goat was not on duty he was usually on the lash in town and I remember he had a liking for a curry in a local restaurant at the end of the evening. Many a time I have witnessed a blind drunk Goat sat in front of a steaming curry and suddenly pass out, falling face first into it, much to the shock of other diners!

Michael Williams 3RTR

"Anyone who has ever made anything of importance was disciplined."
Andrew Hendrixson

Interesting Military Stuff #2. Things you thought you knew about Victoria Crosses.

Ok, here's an easy question that everyone knows the answer to. Where does the metal for VCs come from?
If you said captured Russian guns you are wrong, but it's the answer almost everyone would give.
And here are other things that are 'common knowledge' about the VC.
The VC is the highest award for bravery.
VCs are only awarded to military personnel.
Most VC winners died winning it.
No one has ever won two VCs.
All serving personnel must salute a VC winner.
No woman has ever won a VC.
But every statement above is in fact incorrect. Read on...

Let's start with where the metal to make VCs comes from. If you Google 'Where does the metal for the Victoria Cross come from?' and the quick answer that pops up is, *'The bronze from which all Victoria Crosses are made is supplied by the Central Ordnance Depot in Donnington. This metal is cut from cannons captured from the Russians at Sebastopol during the Crimean War.'*
The location is correct and it's the story we are all familiar with but it's not true. But if you look at the timeline of events you can see why it happened. The story starts when many Russian bronze cannons (probably dozens, but it's hard to pin a number down) were captured at the siege of Sebastopol in September

1855 during the Crimean War and were shipped back to Britain as trophies. Most ended up as prized street ornaments in British cities and some were shipped to commonwealth countries for the same purpose, but a few ended up at the Royal Military Academy Sandhurst and a few more at the Royal Military Academy Woolwich.

The war had been closely followed by the public, long used to Britain being the worlds most militarily powerful country, and had enjoyed poems, paintings, sculptures and of course, newspaper articles about it.

In January 1856 (so only four months after the bronze cannons were captured) the Victoria Cross was introduced by Queen Victoria to honour acts of bravery during the Crimean War and she instructed that it was to be made from bronze. In a fashion that is depressingly familiar to us today a newspaper journalist didn't bother to research things properly and printed a story that said that the bronze used for the VCs was from the Russian guns. Shortly afterwards a letter was printed in the times from a veteran of the war suggesting the same thing.

A legend is made from a simple recipe, a rumour plus time and that is what happened here. As the decades turned into centuries it was passed down and became an unchallenged fact that everyone just 'knew'.

Recent research shows that although Queen Victoria ordered they be cast from bronze, at no time did she specify a source, certainly not the Russian guns. So where is it from? Well, a retired Lieutenant Colonel who did 30 years in the RRF, a Doctor Andrew Marriot has tracked it down.

He used x-ray fluorescence to analyse the composition of Victoria Crosses from 1856 to 2013 and compared it to the composition of Russian cannon from the Crimean War. The results were startling. The early medals were all of a similar composition, but it changed during the First World War and again in the Second World War. And all of them were markedly different from the Russian bronze used to make the Sebastopol cannons.

He also spoke to the London jewellers, Hancocks & Co, who have made every single Victoria Cross since its inception. It turned out that they had been making VCs from a lump of bronze sent to them from the start but after sixty years of making them they started to run out during the First World War and they told the War Office they would soon be needing some more.

I can see the scene clearly in my mind now. Someone in the War Office with a phone in his hand calling across the office, "Dave! Hey Dave! I have Hancocks on the phone!"

"Who?"

"Hancocks! The jewellers who make the Victoria Crosses."

"Oh yeah? What do they want?"

"They say they are running out of bronze for VCs and need some more."

"Where do we get it from?"

"Dunno..."

At this point some smart arse who would be a huge fan of QI if he were alive today would smugly call out, "I know! I know! They are made from Russian cannons captured at the siege of Sebastopol!"

I am pretty sure the staff of the War Office would have been quite busy during the First World War, so some low-ranking minion with a spare afternoon and a hacksaw would have been sent off with a travel warrant and a letter of introduction.

As well as showing that no VCs have ever been made from Russian guns the x-ray studies showed that the metal used for almost all VCs since December 1914 is taken from the cascabel of antique Chinese guns taken as trophies during the first opium War (1839 – 1842). (The cascabel is the round lump at the back end of muzzle loaded cannon.)

The only lump of VC bronze left weighs about 10 kilos and is stored in a secure location at MoD Donnington and may only be removed under armed guard. It has been estimated that there is enough for approximately 85 more VCs.

The second assumption, that the VC is the highest honour has come about because the VC is awarded for bravery '...in the presence of the enemy.' and the George Cross is awarded for bravery '...not in the presence of the enemy.' It was never said that one was lesser than the other, but you can see how it would have been interpreted. The mistake was given a further push when the king said in the speech announcing the award that it should be worn after the Victoria Cross, but this was because it was a later award, not a lesser award.
The George Cross was instituted in 1940 by King George VI because he wanted to be able to reward civilians, for example firemen in the blitz, for bravery even though this bravery was not 'in the presence of the enemy.' This meant that military personnel could also win it if their act of bravery happened 'not in the presence of the enemy.' The confusion has lasted down the years and the current monarch, Queen Elizabeth, confirmed in 2020 that the Victoria Cross and the George Cross are equal in stature.

So if VCs are only awarded for bravery in the presence of the enemy then surely only military personnel can win it? No, that is also not true. It *can* be awarded to civilians too, and seven civilians have won it whilst they were under military command. The last civilian award of the VC happened in 1879 when the Reverend James Williams Adams, a chaplain in the Bengal Ecclesiastical Department saved some lancers who were under fire during the second Afghan war.

But it's so hard to get most people died earning it? Understandable, but another no. There was not a specific instruction when the award was inaugurated, just a general understanding that they would *not* be awarded posthumously.

Instead, their names would be published in the *London Gazette* saying they would have been awarded the Victoria Cross had they survived. Exceptions to this understanding were made during the Boer War and the policy was formally changed in 1907 to allow posthumous awards. The personnel that were gazetted as 'would have won the Victoria Cross' then had the medal sent to their next of kin. There are no lists that say what percentage of recipients died, but it is much lower than 50%. Even during the bloodbath of World War 1 only about one in four were posthumous.

Surely no one has won two? Actually there have been three double winners Captain Charles Upham, Surgeon Captain Arthur Martin-Leake and Captain Noel Chavasse whose stories are so remarkable that I won't attempt to give them here, but recommend you read them in full. Interestingly, Martin-Leake and Chavasse, so two out of the three triple winners were medics.

All serving personnel must salute a VC winner? There is nothing in Queens regs that require this, and nothing in the official warrant, but this tradition has grown up and solidified so even senior officers would salute a private who had been awarded a VC. (This is also true for a winner of a George Cross). Although this sounds really cool, and personally I would feel honoured to just meet a VC winner, imagine you were a private on his way to and from the cookhouse, I think you would get fed up with it pretty quickly.

But surely no woman has won a VC? You could argue this is true, but there is an interesting exception that exists. Elizabeth Webber Harris was married to Webber Desborough Harris, a captain in the 2nd Bengal Fusiliers, and was working as a nurse during a cholera outbreak in India in 1869. The disease was so rampant that the unit was split into two to attempt to control the infection. In three months about one third of the men in Harris's half had died. She nursed the sick, dealt with hostile tribesmen and organised morale boosting activities.

The officers of the 2nd Fusiliers were so impressed that although women were not eligible for the VC, they sought permission from Queen Victoria to award her a solid gold replica Victoria Cross. The Queen assented to this and it was duly awarded by General Sam Browne. The inscription on the back read, 'Presented to Mrs Webber Harris by the officers of the 104th Bengal Fusiliers, for her indomitable pluck, during the cholera epidemic of 1869'.

The rules were changed in 1920 to allow a female to be awarded a VC, but since then none have. Unfortunately the remarkable Harris didn't live to see it, she died in 1917 and her VC is now part of the Ashcroft Collection.

Researched and written by Jonno DP

Fun and games in the field

7 Sigs in Herford (home of the yellow handbags) was, in the 80s, the biggest working unit in the British Army with seven fully manned operational Squadrons and well over 1500 soldiers. It was seen as a bit of a punishment posting, as it virtually always had someone out on exercise, ready to protect the West in case the Russian hordes invaded. My first taste of exercise there was a bit wintry and did not go well for me. We did a night move and had set up the communications node in a German pig farm. (These were all well used for exercise by every Signals unit in Germany at the time). As we had moved in during the night, we had just draped the cam nets on the trucks so come first-light we had to start to finish it properly. I climbed onto the roof of the Electronic Repair Vehicle (ERV) and started to drag the cam net (6 x standard nets knitted together to provide decent cover) so that it was positioned correctly. I went to jump from the box-body roof onto the cab of the bedford and as I did I realised the roof of the cab was covered in ice. I then did a cartoon character slip-slide across the roof and fell off the cab, somehow plummeting in a kneeling position. My left knee hit the bumper of the Bedford and I somersaulted into a pool of freezing (but still semi liquid) pig shit, much to the delight of my comrades Karl, Hank and Twiggy who all laughed, clapped and gave me scores out of 10. My indignity didn't end there. After what felt like a long time lying in pig-shit with blood pissing out of my leg my 'mates' finally stopped laughing at me and I was transported to the nearest Med Centre. When I got there the nurse refused to treat my wound until I had stripped off to my undercrackers and had a shower to wash the shit off. Cheers Florence. I still have a scar on my leg today, 33 years later.

It could have been on the same exercise, but could be months apart, they all tend to merge into one looking back. We moved

into a farm location and had co-located a number of the trucks and I had (without incident), put my cam net up and had it poled out beautifully. Stey Shaw, the Tech Storeman, was on the roof of one of the trucks connecting our cam nets together so we could move between the trucks without messing about and in doing so manged to get some of his buttons stuck in the cam net. As he struggled to move and untangle the buttons, he slipped and fell between the 2 trucks. I heard a large bump on the ERV and went out to investigate. Stey was hanging upside down with a foot and some buttons tangled in the nets swinging gently. "Errr…. can you help Gaz?"
Being the good and loyal mate I am I shouted to Karl, "Hey Karl, come and have a look at Stey."
Karl then shouted to Tony, "Tony, go and grab everyone from the switch."
Stey meanwhile starts to look a little more beetroot, as I get a chair from the back of the truck so I could sit down and take it all in.
"Wankers, the lot of you, just fuckin' get me down."
By the time 15 of us had watched him nearly pass out because he had been upside down for so long, the recce Sergeant wondered what was amusing us all and came and had a look. He gave us the choice of getting him down or stagging on all night.
THUDDD!!
Someone had clambered up and helpfully unhooked a cam net thereby freeing Stey from his anti-gravity device. The downside was I then had to finish off camming up his truck.

Gaz Duffy, Royal Signals (1985-2010)

"In the final choice, a soldier's pack is not so heavy a burden as a prisoner's chains."
Dwight D. Eisenhower

Jacques Cousteau of the RAF

In 1978 the squadron I was serving with went on APC (Armament Practice Camp) to Decimommanu in Sardinia. Unlike nowadays where people fly all the time to exotic places, in 1978 it was rarer and there was great excitement about the trip. We had plenty of free time when we were there and we spent a lot of it on the beautiful beaches drinking, swimming and generally having a great time. There was one guy in the unit who snorkeled and was into wildlife and sea creatures etc. He had talked a lot about getting out in the clear blue waters and seeing what of the local fauna could be found. Every now and then he would come galloping out of the water with tales of fish, other fish, seaweed, sand and the possibility of finding exotic creatures that lurked in the depths. One time he came proudly out of the water holding something in his hand.
"What have you found?" Someone called.
"It's a sea slug!" he called back. "I found it floating on the surface."
Lots of us had no idea what a sea slug was so we clustered around him to have a look. I think doubts had set in, and the snorkeler was less sure of his taxonomy. Everyone studied it in silence for a while until someone said, "It looks like a turd."
"Yeah." Said someone else, "It's a turd."
Well, it turned out they had classified it more accurately than the wannabe Jacques Cousteau had. It was indeed a Richard the Third. Better luck next time mate.

Robert Sayers RAF

Having a hard time

In 1982 myself and the legendary Goat Harris, along with a guy called Mouse, the President of the Bovington Branch of The Nolan Sister's Fan Club, were posted to BATUS. Myself and Mouse were sent to the winter maintenance team and Goat got the job of driver for the Commander of BATUS, who at the time was **an officer from 3RTR.** One night we were in Medicine Hat for a few beers when we decided to go to the Assiniboia Inn (AKA The Sin Bin) where we had heard that there was a male stripper on that night. Why would we want to go to a place with a male stripper you ask? Well, we correctly figured that there would be lots of women of a certain age watching, although we suspected Mouse had other reasons!!

Now, Goat had discovered that on the label of bottles of cough medicine such as actifed and benelyn there was a warning which said **'May cause Drowsiness. Do not drive or operate heavy machinery'** and had discovered that by drinking a whole bottle the effect was like being pissed! Even better, it was much cheaper than buying booze! So prior to our arrival at the Sin Bin (and already pissed) Goat had nipped into a small drug store in the same street where, to his delight, he found what can only be described as a cocktail cabinet of cough medicines. He purchased a couple of bottles which, to the amazement of the man behind the counter, he downed one after the other. Rather unsteadily we made our way into the Sin Bin, sat down right at the edge of the stage and waited.

To loud shrieks of delight the male stripper made his way onto the stage. Mouse also seemed very excited by it all as well as he joined in with the cries of 'Get 'em off' as the stripper started his well-rehearsed routine. From the start the stripper was obviously rather taken by someone on our table as he approached in what you might call a 'semi excited' state. Goat, for reasons known only to him and with a mind befuddled by

beer and cough medicine chasers lent over the railing surround the stage and bit the stripper on the cock. Hard.
There was loud "Aaaaarrrggghhhhh!!!!!!......" from the stripper and a
loud "Ooohhhhhhhhhhh......" from the female crowd. I think Mouse wanted to attempt first aid but we pointed out that the kiss of life wouldn't work.

Michael Williams 3RTR

The Hohne Chronicles part 3. Trade training.

After the Christmas break I had to report to 24th Signal Regiment and train as a Signals Centre Operator which is a little higher qualified than a Teleprinter Operator but less qualified than a Cypher Operator. The course lasted about three weeks and life was a bit easier than the first four of basic training. It was still quite full on, but we were allowed out of camp in the evenings to go to the NAAFI club in Catterick. There were thousands of troops stationed in Catterick and the NAAFI had bars, games rooms, a restaurant, a cinema and a theatre.
The training we did was quite comprehensive. We did the usual drilling and rifle shooting out on the ranges as well, but our trade training included learning army signals procedure, how to type, send and receive messages and all things military. There were guard duties which we had to do about every three weeks to keep the camp safe as the IRA were quite active at the time, so we had to be on our toes. We were also allocated cookhouse duties which consisted of having to work in the cookhouse for a day each month of our stay. This was peeling and eyeing potatoes, washing dishes and any other chores that needed doing.
After the first couple of weeks we were allowed weekend leave if we had been good boys, and this meant getting a leave pass from the course OC. We had an inspection of the barracks every Friday night and we would have to have our kit all laid out on the bed, with our bed packs made up the same as during basic and with the floors bumpered so you could almost see your face in it. The officer of the day would come round and inspect, but if he had had a shit of a day then beware, they could be right bastards. If and when all was satisfactory you could go home for the weekend which most national servicemen did, and the army laid on buses for the soldiers to

most destinations. Mine used to go to Liverpool and then I would have to get the local bus to Ellesmere Port. It became a ritual and every Sunday night it was a case of reversing the process. The buses used to leave from the Liver Building in Liverpool about midnight and get back to Catterick about 4 am. No joke in the winter with three foot of snow on the Yorkshire moors, it was bloody freezing.

We had kit inspection every morning and this meant stripping the bed and folding blankets and sheets into our bed packs. A lot of guys would sleep on the floor so as not to disturb their kit and bed layout. This was very common with those of us returning at such a late hour as it seemed doubly pointless making the bed for just two hours then having to prepare for inspection three or four hours later, we became very resilient. After my three months trade training I passed the Teleprinter Operators course and, as with the selection process for which trade we wanted, we were interviewed and told to choose where we would like to be posted. My options were limited as I was medically categorised as P3 and could only have a home posting. Most of the guys were looking for somewhere exotic to be posted and Britain had troops all around the world back then. I put my name down for a posting to Hong Kong more out of hope than anything else, but whilst refusing me, the army did give me an option. If I was to sign on for an extra year and become a regular, they would waive my P3 status and post me to the Ghurkha Signals in Hong Kong. Strange how that worked. As with many holy men, the mere laying on of hands (or in my case a pen) could change your medical status. If I volunteered to serve an extra year I would instantly become fully fit, but that's the army for you. I declined their kind offer.

L/Cpl J.B. Travers. 207 Signals Squadron. 7th Armoured Brigade 1960/61.

Stupid barista? Stupid bar steward? Or stupid bastard?

As a regiment we would go off camping once a year to get to know each other better. We called them practice camps where we would camp and well... practice stuff. We had a new guy attached to our crew called Mac who was particularly in need of practicing stuff – even making brews. We were the FOOs party (Forward Observation Officer) and were often visited by people who liked to watch explosions, and let's face it, who doesn't?

If you have never been in the Artillery, a battery is split into two unequal groups when live firing. You have the guns, where most of the battery is, sitting around drinking tea waiting for a Fire Mission (These crews were nicknamed, but only at a distance, gun bunnies or trail apes depending on the type of gun), and the OPs (Observation Post) which is a handful of blokes right up at the front directing the fire. (Heroes). If you watch the guns firing, it is almost always indirect fire, which is shooting at something they can't see. So the gun goes 'bang' and that's it, shows over. At the OP end we call up a mission over the radio, tell a gun to fire and see if we hit it. If we don't we 'adjust' the aim of the gun over the radio until it does hit it or gets close enough. Then we get all the guns in the battery to fire simultaneously on the same aim. Explosions aplenty, and a keen sense of competition to see who needs the least goes to be on target. And you don't have to keep putting 50p in the slot.

As this is obviously far more entertaining than being with the guns, we would frequently be visited by people with time on their hands.

One day we were visited by several Senior NCO's and Officers and Mac was sent off to make teas and coffees. Half our visitors wanted tea, and half coffee, so Mac was told, "Six brews, half tea, half coffee." After a bit he comes back and our esteemed visitors start sipping their delicious hot beverages.

"Here, I think I have got your coffee."

"Uhh.. no, I think this one's coffee."

"I think this one's tea, but it tastes funny."

They went around and around the mulberry bush for a bit and we decided to ask Mac back to ID the drinks.

"Which is which Mac?"

"Uh?"

"Which is tea and which is coffee?"

"They all are."

Suppressing the urge to beat him to death a Sergeant Major said a bit more forcefully "Which fucking drinks are coffee, and which ones are tea?"

Mac looked sheepish and said, "They are all tea and coffee. You said half tea half coffee..."

Give that man two medals!!!

Gunner 'X' RA

"If serving is beneath you, leadership is beyond you."
Jerome Gay Jr.

Sometimes you have to make your own amusement in the Falklands

In 1992 I finished my Royal Signals class 1 trade course and was posted, as 80 % of us were, to a six-month tour in the Falkland Islands. I was posted to the FI Systems Control, part of the Joint Comms Unit, JCUFI. On arrival, I was greeted by the guy I was replacing and he shoved a can in my hand with the words, "You're already behind, you fucking lightweight," and so it went on for the next 7 months.

Night shifts were particularly boring, as not much happened unless a flight was due to arrive, so we found ourselves with shit jobs to complete and time on our hands. On one of the night shifts, we had an idea. We could prank call people! We had control of the exchanges and could turn off the call logging machine. We also knew how to carry out certain tricks during the call to allow us to choose certain trunk routes to make calls, thereby stopping any tracing (which we would be tasked to do anyway).

06:30. Bored. Very bored indeed.

We knew the Commander British Forces Falkland Islands (CBFFI – 'SeeBiffy') had arrived at the HQ across the road as his vehicle was in its slot and the lights were on. Pick up phone, select an outgoing trunk to one telephone exchange, then another, then another, dial CBFFI's number and wait for the answer.

"Good morning, Commander British Forces"

"Morning sir, do you know who this is?"

"No."

"Well fuck off then!" Slam down phone, roar with laughter! Repeat on the next night shift and if really bored again on the day shift.

After a few weeks of this CBFFI got his best Royal Signals technicians in to find out who was doing the prank calls. Us. Trenny (nickname only as he's a serving Lieutenant Colonel) gets called across to the commanders office to devise a plan for 'catching the little shits'. A hot-line phone is installed between the commander's office and the Monarch desk (which was in the same room as my desk), for the purpose of initiating a call trace. Needless to say, Trenny played the game. When I prank called CBFFI he got the call to initiate the trace. He would roll his eyes at me and say to CBFFI on the phone, "Just keep them on the line sir, I'm logging into the next exchange". At this point I would end the call with, "You still don't know me, so fuck off!" Our little game came to an end when I got a bit too casual and nearly got caught. Trenny got the hot-line call and during it he could hear my laughter echoing down the line, as CBFFI had the call on speaker. We knew, but CBFFI didn't seem to have worked it out, that the only way this could happen was if I was physically near to Trinny. I was laughing my head off as the poor commander was trying his best to keep me talking as I was telling him to fuck off for the last time.

Shenanigans didn't stop there. The Royal Signals techs carried out a secondary task to help out BFBS/SSVC. We were the Videotape and Teletext operators who cued up and changed the transmission tapes. We also updated the teletext pages and instant messages, thus, providing entertainment for everyone on the Falklands and passing on useful information and getting a few quid as a reward. It was far cheaper than BFBS having their own VT operators there, I can tell you. Two things happened whilst we had control of this that could be classed as noteworthy.

The first was having access to the studios. We were dicking around in an off-air radio booth and found that the competition jingles and questions were pre-recorded and kept on a tape in the studio ready for the following morning. Excellent! We would listen to the questions, go away and find the answers and let the guys who would be on shift know what they were. We won a lot of BFBS pen sets and round-things (these round things were actually a bottle opener/seal – why they needed the seal was beyond me, who would leave half a beer??).

Then we went to the next level. They did a competition where the prizes were a meal voucher for the pub in Stanley. Remember, we had control of the phone system. Once we had identified valid opposition for the phone-ins we would deactivate their phone just as the questions were being read out. On one occasion we diverted all of BFBSs calls to one of our other phones which we obviously left unanswered, then connected ourselves to BFBS and answered the questions. Yummy!

The second was during the 1992 general election. It was the first time that the Falklands had a live broadcast of an election and we were called on to monitor the satellite feed and its re-broadcast. Watty (I think it's Mark Watts, but not entirely sure as I only ever called him Watty) was fiddling with the teletext machine. You could type a message and preview what it would look like on a TV set if it was broadcast. During a speech given by the then Prime Minister John Major, he typed in 'What a boring bastard' and set it to scroll along the bottom of the screen. He called me across and said, "Hey, look at this! Funny as fuck!" Unfortunately, he inadvertently hit the transmit key and it went out to everyone. I don't think the second scroll had started when the incoming lines at the studio lit up. The head of BFBS for the Falklands was not a happy man and Watty was banned from doing TV for a month!

On a visit by Maggie Thatcher commemorating the ten-year anniversary of the liberation she was accompanied by Terry Waite who, as you probably remember, was held hostage by terrorists for four years. One of the guys got in before me and asked him, "So was it still there, when you got back?" He took it in good spirit and said, no, it had been removed. He was referring to the typically squaddie style joke 'What's black and rusty and sits outside Westminster Abbey?' Answer - Terry Waites bike! Boom!

The communications centre (Comcen) was manned mostly by female operators who used to get out of their uniform and wear sports kit on the night shift. This used to piss us off as we were forbidden from getting out of uniform as we were the ones that had to go through to the Joint Operations Centre (JOC) if there were any comms issues. One shift whilst the Comcen wasn't very busy, I went through to ask a question and everyone besides the desk operator was asleep. I quietly picked up the stacks of neatly folded uniform and took it all into the corridor between the SYSCON and Comcen and proceeded to staple each uniform to the wall with an industrial stapler complete with shoes and hats as if they were all stood at ease. At 6 in the morning there were some very unhappy ladies in the COMCEN, none more so than my 'shifty' Jim Robertson's wife, whose uniform was one of those stapled to the wall. We (Jim and myself) both found it highly amusing watching them try to get their uniform off the wall and back into it before the higher ups started arriving.

Gaz Duffy, Royal Signals (1985-2010)

It's a riot!

I left the 2nd Royal Tank Regiment in May 1970 so this story must have happened in 1969. The 'troubles' in Ireland had started. John Hume and Bernadette Devlin were leading civil rights marches through the streets of Belfast and Londonderry and many of these marches ended in violent confrontations between the police and demonstrators. The Army were given the thankless task of supporting the police and providing a buffer zone between the Protestant and Catholic communities. As a result, each Regiment was requested to recruit and train a detachment of soldiers that would be trained as infantry in the techniques of riot control.

Thirty or forty of us signed up with little thought of the consequences, but more as a means of relieving the drudgery of peace-time soldiering. We were blessed with a couple of instructors from the Sherwood Foresters, who, by military standards, were quite sympathetic to us 'tankies'. After all, we were never really subject to the rigours of infantry training, a ten-mile bash once a year was usually the limit of our fitness regime.

We watched grainy black and white film taken during the Malayan Emergency where British troops developed the techniques we were about to experience. The first reel might have been to show 'How to Confront an Angry Crowd with Poise and Dignity,' and not much else. Only the British Army could come up with a plan like this – it didn't work at Rorkes Drift, so I couldn't imagine for a moment that it would work on the streets of Belfast, but this is how it went.

We were split up into two sections. About a dozen of us were designated troops and the rest became a baying crowd of angry protesters. Two of us carried the poles of a banner and we were to march in good order with empty magazines up to the front of the crowd. We would then form up in two ranks facing the crowd with the banner carriers to our rear. At a word of command, the front rank would kneel and the two guys at the back would unfurl the banner which said something like, "Please disperse or we will be forced to open fire," in whatever language was applicable to the crowd. If this didn't work, and our hopes weren't high, our officer was supposed to calmly walk along our ranks and place a single bullet next to each one of us. They would all be blanks... except one!

On another command, we would each load the bullet, and if this failed to intimidate the rioters, we were ordered to aim for one of the ringleaders, say, the man with the red hat, and on the command 'Fire' we would shoot the silly bugger.

The theory was that none of us would know who shot the fatal bullet, but the Self-Loading Rifle cocks itself using back pressure from a bullet leaving the barrel. A blank round does not create this pressure so the reality would have been that only one rifle would have 'self-loaded', and the firer would have known whether it was a blank or not, but I suppose nobody thought of that. Anyway, after that, the rioters would all run away and we would march off again in good military order leaving peace, goodwill and just the one dead body behind us.

The writer Bernard Cornwell describes in his tales of Vikings and King Arthur, about what it was like to fight in a shield wall and does so far more eloquently than I could. The second phase of our training was the closest a modern soldier would get to that experience.

Once again, we were divided into two groups. One group were the troops, the other became the mob. They were issued with handfuls of water-soaked cotton waste to throw at us. Just as an aside, I've never seen what we called cotton waste outside the army. It would arrive by the sack load and consisted of off-cuts of cotton thread all bundled together in one big multi-coloured clump and would normally be used to mop up oil spills etc. My group were issued with three-quarter length riot shields and pick-axe handles – light enough to swing, but heavy enough to cause a lot of damage to flesh and bone. We were required to form up in two ranks and face the mob, who in turn were instructed to make themselves obnoxious, shouting, swearing and lobbing big wet clods of waste at us.

We would advance slowly with shields touching, and the front rank would try to push the crowd back. If this failed, we would retire about a metre and switch to plan B, and this is where Bernard Cornwell's description came to life. On command, we would rush back at the crowd and with shields held high, bend at the waist and swinging the pickaxe handles underneath to crack shins and anything else - in the same way the old Saxons would have done using swords. Nothing could withstand that sort of attack. In a live situation, broken legs and severe injury would have been a distinct probability.

The downside of this procedure was that it was physically draining, and after just twenty or thirty seconds, the front rank would retire to catch their breath, and the second rank would take over. By leap frogging like this, even a large crowd could be moved along and dispersed quite easily. However, Bernard Cornwell would tell you that there was one flaw in this plan. Unless it took place in a confined space, typically a street environment, the crowd would outflank the troops and you would be truly in the brown stuff.

The third phase was all about booby traps. In urban style warfare, booby traps are a constant menace. Anything that can be stood on, tripped over, or picked up could be attached by a fine wire or fishing line to something that might make a really loud bang. We were shown all sorts of devices; pressure on, pressure off, trip wires and so on, attached to anything from the innocuous, like a shoe, to something desirable like a watch, even a can of coke.

Somewhere in the heart of Luneburg Heath, was a deserted and derelict farmhouse. For all I know, it had been like that since the war when NATO took over the area for troop training. We were transported there in three ton trucks in order to search the premises for terrorists who might be hiding in the building. When we got there, it was a huge rambling house, no glass in the boarded up windows and all the doors askew. A quick survey from outside showed that all the rooms were littered with debris, a perfect environment for deadly booby traps.

We split into several teams, each entering gingerly through different doorways, some turning left, others turning right. Inside it was dark and dingy, quite creepy in fact. All the while looking for trip wires we advanced down a corridor checking out rooms as we went. The first room looked OK, no strange men, watches, or cans of coke. The second room though, looked decidedly dodgy. The ceiling had caved in, and planks of wood and debris littered the floor, such that we couldn't go inside without moving some of it. By this time, we heard explosions from the other side of the building, indicating to us that some of the other teams had hit problems.

Unable to see any wires but still unwilling to move anything, we decided to do the next best thing. So using the dividing wall as a barrier, we lobbed a big chunk of wood into the room to dislodge the debris and………. BOOOOOM!!!!, a big pyrotechnic explosion battered our eardrums as it echoed round that confined space. To this day, I wonder if that dividing wall would have been enough to shield us had that been a real booby trap – probably not.

We continued our slow advance along the corridor. To our left was a stairway up to the first floor which we were told was too dangerous to search. As we passed, it became darker - very dark. I know this because as I passed the underside of the stairs, I looked, then looked again. I could barely make out the hooded figure dressed in black, crouching in the darkness. For what might have been just a few seconds but seemed like ages I was dead. The figure rose and moved toward me – and I still hadn't twigged what it was. It was one of our old friends from the Sherwood Foresters and he just handed himself over, but if

he had something more dramatic in mind, I had been a sitting duck.
So our official training ended; the Sherwood Foresters returned to their units, and we went back to our regular day jobs.

Gordon Simmonds 2RTR

Now *that* Is Discipline!

In 1981-82 I was CSM of No2 company 1st Battalion Welsh Guards (1WG) who were stationed at Elizabeth Barracks, Pirbright. The training WO was a colleague of mine called Ernie Pritchard and he owned a large hairy black and white Welsh Collie dog which he brought to work most days. All company offices were part brick and part wooden with doors at the center of the building with a small hallway inside with offices either side.

Ernie always left his office door open, but his dog would react to all noise such as a phone ringing or a door being opened so he put a large coffee table to the left of his office door and whenever his dog reacted to noise Ernie would shout a command, "Lie down!" and the dog would go and lie under the table.

One day when the dog had been particularly restless and I heard Ernie repeatedly telling it to settle down, a guardsman arrived at his office with a message. As readers who served will be aware, many regiments and corps have their own particular customs and idiosyncrasies. (I had to Google the spelling of this word as I might have typed 'Idiot Sin Cities'.) In the Guards, when a junior rank approaches a senior NCO or officer he or she will halt and stand to attention which is referred to as 'putting your feet in'.

So the guardsman came into the office and put his feet in with a 'Bang! Bang!' This disturbed the dog and he got up to have a look. Seeing this an exasperated Ernie shouted, "Get under the fucking table!" and finished what he was writing.

After he was done Ernie looked up to see an empty room. Wondering if he was going bonkers, he asked himself if he had imagined it, but he realized that the dog was not under the table. It kept looking under the table, then at him, then under the table, then back at him. Ernie raised himself off his seat slightly so he could see under the coffee table, and there was the missing guardsman.

As lesser mortals are probably aware, discipline in the guards is legendary and even Ernie was impressed by the immediate and instinctive reaction. Maybe not so impressed with his common sense though...

RSM James Everett Welsh Guards

Under the Wildlife and Countryside Act it is explicitly illegal to kill a hedgehog with a machine gun. (This is true, I checked it – Jonno DP)

In the shit

When I was a newly posted Gunner to an RA Field Regiment in West Germany I got put on my first (of many, too many) guard duties. I was doing that exciting bit of being on the gate at around midnight. You know, the stag where a squirrel climbing a tree is a welcome distraction.

The silence of the camp was broken by a strange sound coming from the Royal Signals side of the barracks. It was the distant echoing of an approaching NCO shouting the hoarse commands 'eft-ight-eft-ight-eft-ight......." at double time. After a while the producer of the noise came out of the gloom and continued to approach the guardroom. It was a scene so peculiar and unexpected at midnight I actually wondered if I was imagining in it. It was two Regimental Police either side of a stark bollock naked soldier who was doing his best to keep time. I carried on observing the spectacle whilst the soldier was marking time so the door could be opened, and what a fine soldierly sight he was. Then the three entered the guard room and the shouting recommenced from the cell passageway.

After the stag finished I naturally made enquiries as to what the naked soldier had done in order to be paraded in such a manner down the main regimental strasse. It transpired that the poor signalman had got himself wasted in the old Colonel Gaddafi and had broken into the officers mess through a window. What made the offence slightly more serious was that he had taken a shit on the window ledge and had undressed and gone for a kip in a fresh bed prepared for senior visiting officer expected to arrive in the morning. Ahhhh... The old days eh?

Gunner X. Royal Artillery.

Love will find a way

From 1982 to 1987 I was a brat living in Brackel near Dortmund as my dad was in HQ Battery 22 Air Defence Regiment RA. In the summer of 1983 there was this girl who lived near us called Sara Foster and my friend Matthew Smith absolutely fancied the arse off her. Her dad was due to be posted back to England soon so we decided to go into Dortmund city centre to get her a leaving present but there was a snag, no money. So it was a shoplifting spree rather than a shopping spree.

Me and Matt were 13 and my younger brother Lee was 11, so Oceans 8 it wasn't. The first couple of shoplifts went smoothly but then we got greedy and decided to nick a watch from the German Woolworths, and yes, we got caught. Like the hardened criminals we were though, we had thought it all through and had very cool false names at the ready to baffle the police. I chose the name Joe Strummer, who was the then very famous guitarist in the Clash, who at that time were at the height of their stardom.

We were kept at the back of the shop until the German Polizei came to question us, but we put into action the second part of our plan. We kept saying we were British and the military police should be informed that we'd been stopped. The German police tried a bit of strong arm tactics but we stood firm and told them get the MPs in.

The MPs turned up and drove us to the cells in camp 7 where they left us to stew for an hour. All of our overinflated bravado had pretty much evaporated by this point and worse, I wasn't sure they believed I was Joe Strummer.

After what felt like years some of the huge and scary MPs came into the cell and one of them said, "Right! We have had a word with your dads and we've agreed on a suitable punishment for thieving little bastards like you!"

That's when I really started to panic. At that time MPs did not exactly have a reputation for being sweet natured and my imagination started to work overtime on what terrible punishment would be meted out to us. I hoped we wouldn't have to do maths lessons in prison.
"Hold your fucking hands out now!"
We instantly did as we were told and were sweating piss as we watched him pick up his pace stick and hold it over our soft little palms. We closed our eyes and clenched our whole bodies, waiting for the agonising pain that was coming.
We felt the slightest little taps on our hands and the heard the words "Don't do it again! You're banned from Woolies for a year!" And then a massive laugh from the room full of MPs.
Due to our little foray into the world of crime my friendship with Matt was cut short as his dad, a Bombardier in 19 Field Regiment, blamed me and my brother for it all. Mind you, Matt didn't get off scott free. He was shipped off to boarding school so he wouldn't be able to hang around with undesirables!

Mark Townsend

It's good to talk

Exercises in Germany could be on the long side for a busy Signal Regiment, so one evening during the trip back from the resupply run to the detachments, I asked my best mate Karl to stop near a phone box so I could give home a quick ring. With a smile, he said, "What do you need a phone box for? We are Signals and I have the butt phone (used to test telephone lines) in the back of the rover."

So we started looking at the Bundespost telegraph poles to find one with a junction box on it. After a bit we found one in a relatively remote location and parked the land rover amongst some trees and pulled the ladders off the top. I went up, opened the junction box and listened into the pairs of wires until I got a dial-tone. Then I unscrewed and disconnected them simultaneously to stop the phone in the nearby Germans house from 'tinkling' (this is the person who's bill it would appear on). I connected some don 10 and dropped it to the bottom of the pole. We hooked up the butt phone and both had a lovely chat with home, then reversed the process, removing the don 10. I wonder how many Germans had blazing rows with members of their family after receiving big telephone bills with international calls on them. Luckily, this was way before itemised billing, so they possibly just had to argue who was calling whom!

Gaz Duffy, Royal Signals (1985-2010)

A couple of great ideas

Sometimes mankind makes a huge leap forward when someone thinks totally 'outside the box' and sometimes (in this case 1990 in a laundry room in Northern Ireland) two gunners have a conversation like this.
"How long do you think I can stay in that tumble dryer?"
"Dunno."
After a few minutes and a number of spin-thud – spin-thud – spin-thuds the Gunner was rescued from the industrial sized machine after realising this was after all, not one of the worlds greatest experiments. He was then sick on the floor and took a surprising amount of time to fully recover.
That Great Minds are seldom found in the lower ranks of the army was demonstrated to me once again on a night exercise in Soltau back in '91. The infantry were gathered for debrief by their CSM, and we (the FOOs party) were in there too. All of a sudden the Sergeant Major shouts to one of his Rifleman, "WHO SAID YOU COULD SMOKE??!!"
The startled rifleman replied, "My Mum when I was sixteen."

Gunner X. Royal Artillery.

The Hohne Chronicles part 4. Posting.

I was posted to, and eventually arrived at, 1 Division Signals Regiment in Verden on the river Aller in Lower Saxony in Germany around the end of March 1960. I was one of several woolly battle-dressed National Servicemen. We were fully trained and raring to go, but it was 'paint this, clean that, weed this' and many other general duties that squaddies get in a Signals Regiment. I was in Oscar Troop which comprised of about forty operators, but the signals office only required about six to function. The rest of us were just kept occupied, sweeping up, cleaning up and painting anything that didn't move, and saluting anything that did.

One day out of the blue I was given orders to pack my kit and go to 207 Signals Squadron in Hohne on Luneburg Heath. Me and another signalman called Derek Kelly from Glasgow (I would love to know where he is now and what he's doing) climbed onto a truck and we were taken to the 4th Regiment

Royal Horse Artillery where we were to be rationed and quartered.

Me and Jock outside the Signal Centre 1960

I had heard about the bullshit of the Guards Regiments, but this outfit, 4th RHA would have taken some beating. (I can believe this – I was 3rd RHA – Jonno DP).

We were only with the RHA for food and lodgings, our actual unit for admin and discipline was 40 miles away in Soltau, so admin wise we kept our distance from them. After reporting to HQ Battery block and giving them all our details we were allocated a two-man room. Wow! What luxury! After the five-minute settling in period we were directed to our place of work which was a small signal centre at the end of the Post Office building the Post office being run by the Royal Engineers.

We went over to meet the Signals Detachment which consisted of two Corporal Cipher Operators, two Sigcen Operators and two teleprinter operators. Derek and I were the replacements for the two Sigcen Operators, who were due for demob and they didn't hang around. By the time me and Derek got there they had already left.

Hohne camp itself was huge. It was a transit camp for a lot of units training as part of NATO and there was also a lot of units permanently stationed there. When I was there we had a Regiment of the QRIH, 26 Armoured Engineer Squadron, 4th Regiment RHA, a squadron of 14/20th Kings Hussars, all the support services for these units, medics, schools and married quarters. It had its own cinema, YMCA, and a huge NAAFI shop for the married families. Really, it was a town in its own right. As well as all the British troops, NATO had a Headquarters with various admin staff stationed there to cater for the visiting training regiments.

We had several great fiddles going on around the camp selling stuff to the locals. Next door in the Army Post Office, an MSO driver (displaced person from the war) would come to pick up the mail from the camp each night and we would sell him our duty-free ciggies, but we had an even better fiddle going. We would pick up dry rations from the cook house, for our night shifts and this would include bread, butter and a large can or jar of Nescafe coffee. The Germans were still drinking what they called ersatz (replacement) coffee as war austerities were still in place but this undrinkable muck was made from ground hazelnut shells and flavour added to make it taste like coffee. It didn't. I would walk over to the NAAFI and see my friend Anna, slip her the can of coffee, and she would pass me a couple of cartons of cigarettes which I would sell to the MSO driver. It was quite a serious offence if you ever got caught, and the fine was quite severe. For every cigarette you were caught selling the cost was one Deutschmark per cigarette, so for a carton of 200 say, it would cost you 200 marks which was approximately eight weeks wages.

Of course we still had some army discipline to contend with but we didn't really take to it. I remember the day when I was told I was going to be promoted to lance corporal. This Royal Signals Sergeant who none of us had ever met turns up out of the blue and asks, "Who is in charge?"

I looked around the room, we were all privates.

"You are." I said.

"No, you are. Go to the stores and get yourself a stripe, you are now a lance corporal." With this momentous announcement, he left. It was a simple as that. He hung around for about two weeks after which we never saw him again the lazy bastard. I was now in charge of the day to day running of the Sigcen. The Cypher corporals were given their rank because of the responsibility they had as Cypher Operators, but basically I had to run the place. Goodness me, a wage increase, or so I thought. I was paid an extra three shillings and six pence per week, hooray! But the RHA charged me four shillings a week for Corporals mess fees! Ah!

We used to get a ring from Brigade or Division telling us to switch on the teleprinters and it was usually a Noticas (Notification of Casualties) message for the War Office informing us that someone had been killed on the autobahn or on exercise, but the night of the 13th August 1961 it was something else! This was the night that the East Germans closed the border between East and West Berlin and started building The Wall. I got the call to open up the circuit and the bells started to ring. I was instructed to ring every orderly room and get their despatch riders or orderlies down post-haste. The messages were passed on and the movement of units began. The whole camp started to empty and move out down the road. This went on for a long time before the stand down was given. I tell you it was full on, and a lot of squaddies were killed that night in accidents, the whole of NATO was on the move, and in a hurry.

The powers that be thought it could the start of something big, possibly the start of World War III, I kid you not. I had a confrontation with a Major from 4th RHA who saw me standing in the doorway of the Sigcen and demanded that I evacuate the place immediately.

"Don't you know the Russians are coming?" he barked.

I tried to explain to his brain cell that I was the one who had given him the message in the first place and I even ended up having to get abusive and threaten him with a pick handle when he tried to force me to leave. I rang my officer at 7th Armoured Brigade HQ, which in those days was in Celle, to explain the situation. He just told me to keep out of the way for a few days until the guy could be straightened out and I never heard any more about it. The flap was over in a couple of days.

L/Cpl J.B. Travers. 207 Signals Squadron. 7th Armoured Brigade 1960/61.

1968 was the only year in the 20th century when no member of the British armed services was killed on active service.

Pulling the pin

The officers of Royal Signals Corps Main decided to have an Officers Mess function in the field and soldiers were requested from each of the comms nodes to provide the staff to be waiters. Bearing in mind we had been out in the field for weeks and hadn't been given any shower runs at all, we were all transported back to camp to have a shower and get some barrack dress. We then had to wait on the officers whilst they had a stupendous meal, wine, port, the works. And to add insult to injury we were forbidden from scoffing any leftovers. I was annoyed and, like many others, I took a dump in an officers ammo pouch. The guys who were based at Corps Main took it a bit further. Well, quite a lot further to be honest.

The HQ trucks were interconnected by a large platform that was built between the backs of all of the B-Staff vehicles, secured by chains to the vehicles with legs underneath, a bit like a stage. After the dinner night the lads were pretty pissed off so they came up with an idea that they would unpin all of the legs and remove the chains making the platform between all of the trucks a floating jigsaw of metal tailgates and platforms. To encourage the Rodneys into the trap someone suggested they switch off the generator thus plunging the officers into darkness and encouraging them to come out and see what had happened. SAS we are not, but the plan was executed perfectly and it worked like a dream. Well oiled pins were silently removed and chains gently lifted off. Lovely. Part A complete, the generator stop button was hit and officers started pouring out of their vehicles. Plummy accents abounded.

"Fawman! Fawman! Where's the powah? The lights have gone orf!"

About 30 seconds later the jigsaw collapsed leaving a pile of entangled and furious officers, a few of whom needed hospital treatment. A short investigation quickly indicated sabotage by the underlings and for two whole days the troops stood outside in all weathers whilst the officers waited for someone to own up. I'm glad to say nobody cracked and the officers realised that if they wanted to continue the exercise they would need their soldiers to do their actual jobs so with numerous threats and promises the matter was dropped. I wasn't involved in this (honestly) but two of my close friends were involved in the 'un-pinning'.

Gaz Duffy, Royal Signals (1985-2010)

Interesting military stuff # 3. The Charge of the Light Brigade and why it still matters.

The charge of the Light Brigade is one of those things that most people have heard of but few, even military or ex-military could tell you much about. It was a battle in the Crimean war, a war which Britain and France fought against Russia from October 1853 to February 1856 and has quite rightly passed into legend. Not just one legend. Three legends.

The cause of the Crimean war was relatively straightforward and centred around the declining Empire of the Ottoman Turks, which by the mid-19th century was no longer the dominant middle eastern power it used to be. The possibility that the entire Ottoman Empire may collapse was noticed by tsar Nicholas of Russia, (the great-grandfather of the one who was shot during the Communist Revolution) and he saw this as a golden opportunity to expand his own Russian empire in general and seize control of some warm water ports in particular, something the Russians still sought to do during the Cold War.

Look at a map of Russia and you will see a surprising fact for a country that covers around one tenth of all the land on planet Earth. Her huge coastline is almost entirely far to the North and therefore icebound during the winter. She has a Pacific Coast which is not ice bound, but of course for any war in Europe, Pacific ports are useless. The only permanently ice-free ports Russia had (and has) near Europe are in the Black Sea and to make good use of this fact the Russians built a massive naval base at Sevastopol on the Crimean Peninsula. Unfortunately for the Russians geography has as made this less than perfect. The Black Sea is almost completely landlocked with only one tiny exit into the Mediterranean and the land both sides of this exit is owned by Turkey. At some points the passage is narrow as 750 metres so bottling up a Russian fleet wishing to leave the Black Sea would be a simple matter for the Turks. So capturing this narrow straight would mean the Russians were free to come and go at will from the Black Sea and also they would have a warm water port closer to Europe and Africa.

It easy to criticise the Russians for this shameless opportunism, but the British are not exactly in a position to criticise others for empire building. The empire we had was the biggest the world has ever seen and was almost double the size of the Russian one at its largest extent. And in any case, at this time all the European powers were playing what was called 'The Great Game'. Britain, France, Russia and others were all trying to expand their Empires as much as possible whilst worrying about their rivals getting in first. So as is often the case in high politics, it's not that one side necessarily wants it, it was just they didn't want the other side to have it.

Even the Tsar of Russia couldn't just invade countries without an excuse, but fortunately for him, one was provided. The Tsar liked to promote himself as the protector of the worlds orthodox Christians and at the same time the then leader of France, who was the nephew of Napoleon Bonaparte, (and who was calling himself Napoleon the third) made similar claims about the worlds Catholics.

The reality was that neither gave a shit about these people quietly minding their own business, it was just a political excuse to steal someone else's territory. We *have* been here before. If you served in the British Army from 1969 to 1990, whether you served in op banner or not you are probably thinking, 'Fucking religion again!' Anyway, in 1853 a riot broke out in Jerusalem Between Catholic and Orthodox monks around access to the church of the Holy sepulchre. Just to pause for a minute, hands up who would like to see it, just for the curiosity value, a riot organised by monks? Yes, me too.

In the end several Orthodox Christians were left dead, the tsar feigned outrage and delightedly massed his troops on the border. Turkey was seriously rattled by this and went to Britain and France asking for help but then the Turks (and it still isn't well understood why they did this) rather rashly declared war on Russia.

The British and French didn't jump in straight away as they were hoping the Turks could hold off the Russians on their own but after a catastrophic Turkish naval defeat in November Anglo-French involvement was virtually guaranteed. By March the following year the British press had been become completely gripped with war fever and the newspaper editors in their comfortable offices would accept nothing less than British intervention and therefore a decisive victory. (We have been here before too.)

The French declared war on Russia on March the 26th and Britain followed suit a day later. At this point you may be wondering why it was called the Crimean war rather than something like the Anglo-Russian war. the reason is because all of the action took place on the Peninsula of the Crimea, which was then part of Russia, and is again now after they annexed it (a posh diplomatic word for nicked) from the independent country of Ukraine.

The allied plan was to land a force on the Crimean Peninsula, capture the large port of Sebastopol and therefore remove almost all Russian naval capability in the region. If the allies held that key port then the British and French navies would be able to easily dispose of any Russian forces operating against Turkey. This strategy was sound enough but the implementation of it can only be described as shambolic. the Allied invasion was disorganised and poorly planned but worst of all badly managed on the ground. This was the first military campaign fought by the British since the death of the Legendary Duke of Wellington (the guy who beat Napoleon at

Waterloo) and you get the feeling that no one had really filled his shoes. (Or wellies I suppose we should say).

So profound was the loss of the so-called Iron Duke that even Prince Albert described the British Army without his leadership as merely a collection of regiments rather than an army. Without his deft touch and organisational flair all sort of cock ups were taking place. Boats were dropping the kit in the wrong places or turning up with kit that was no longer serviceable. For example, horses were left on a ship for so long they died and there was at least one case of British soldiers starving to death while huge stockpiles of food rotted on a beach two miles away. The Crimean war was an ungodly mess of poor planning, squandered chances and needless bloodshed. It's illuminating therefore, to have a quick look at the main players in charge. If you thought your officers were a bit weird, strap in, these guys are raving.

By the way, it was about this time that a phrase that has been used many times since started doing the rounds. This phrase was, "The British soldiers fought like lions, but they were led by donkeys." This phrase has been reused many times and has been attributed to many people including Erwin Rommel, probably the famoustest German general in World War II. Who knows if it was genuinely used during the Crimean war but without doubt it was true.

Donkey number one was the overall commander on the ground, Lord Raglan. By 1854 Lord Raglan has had a long and distinguished military career including being the Duke of Wellington's military secretary throughout the Napoleonic Wars. During these wars Raglan had distinguished himself for bravery and had even lost his right arm to a French gun during the Battle of Waterloo. but despite this he had always been the efficient assistant to the visionary Lord Wellington, rather than a great leader in his own right. After Wellington died Raglan was his natural successor, but he was nothing like the general he had served. By the time he got to the Crimean war whatever talents Raglan may have had seem to have faded. For a start he was sixty-five and had never once led men in the field himself. Also, his eyesight was deteriorating and so it was often difficult for him to see what was going on the battlefield. There is also a possibility that his mental faculties were failing, for example he kept getting confused about who was actually involved in the war and kept referring to the Russians as the French. Many historians think that this story is not true, but they are universally in agreement that Raglan was a terrible general. He issued confusing and often vague orders and failed to capitalise on golden opportunities.

Donkey number two was George Bingham, AKA Lord Lucan who had overall command of the cavalry. Over 100 years later, in 1974, one of his descendants would famously murder his nanny and fuck off sharpish, never to be seen again. Lord Lucan was 54 years old when he went out to the Crimea and was the commanding officer of the 17th Lancers, one of the most distinguished cavalry regiments in the British Army. At the start of the campaign he was named as the overall commander of the cavalry division. This impressive title suggests he had an illustrious military career, but this is not the case. He had bought his commission in the army (common at the time) and then used a trick that many people did to get promoted. Essentially he would buy the next rank and then go on to half pay and wait until an opportunity came to buy the next rank and then he would go back on half pay again. So although he had a high rank he had very little military experience. To modern ears this sounds like an insane idea of how to recruit officers, but the reasoning behind it is understandable. If the upper class commanded the army than the army could not become a threat to the upper class. The not-so-long-ago French Revolution had succeeded at least partly because the revolutionaries had gained the support of middle-class Army officers who had risen to their positions on merit. British aristocrats were not about to allow that situation to develop in Britain, so officer status was closed to all but the toffs.

By the time Lucan was in charge of the cavalry division in the Crimean war he had never really led men and had leapfrogged over many talented and experienced officers who had served for decades, including some who had fought during the Napoleonic Wars. Even amongst the many talentless rich who filled the officer ranks of the cavalry, Lucan was particularly disliked. He spent a great deal of his own money equipping his men in fancy uniforms which made them targets of ridicule from other soldiers and he quickly gained a reputation for cruelty, often inflicting brutal punishments on his men for the tiniest of misdemeanours. For example, if he found any of his men with even a small part of his uniform out of order he would have him publicly flogged. Here he was building on a reputation he had started when he was unnecessarily cruel to his tenant farmers during the potato famine in Ireland, and the abuse of his wife which was common knowledge amongst his peers. This abuse of his wife meant that his wife's brother, Lord Cardigan, had a particular hatred for him which even the Duke of Wellington had failed to reconcile.

During the Crimean war this was a major problem because the third donkey *was* Lord Cardigan.

James Brundell, the 7th Earl of Cardigan was the commander of the light brigade and is such a strange character it's hard to believe that he had actually existed. He often seems like a cartoon version of a nineteenth-century British aristocrat. He was vain, petty, arrogant, and seemed to take a particular delight in humiliating his subordinates. Like his brother-in-law, Lord Lucan, he had risen to his position not because of talent but by the same trick of purchasing his promotions until he found himself in charge of the light brigade. His facial hair is spectacular, by the way. He looks like someone who has put on a fake moustache to take the piss.

Lord Cardigan spending quality time with his facial hair. Gorgeous.

Lord Cardigan had always had a reputation for being stupid and mean. As a child he had fallen from a horse and banged his head, and his family often said he'd never been right ever since. Once he had an officer court-martialled for ordering stable jackets that he didn't like. (Stable jackets that Cardigan himself had chosen.) The court-martial ruled the Cardigan was acting unfairly, threw the charge out and relieved him of his command. But because of the system of purchasing promotions Cardigan was soon back in command of another regiment. Perhaps the best example of Lord Cardigans pettiness and stupidity was demonstrated by the so-called black bottle incident. One night the Inspector General of the cavalry and his staff were dining at Cardigans mess. Cardigan had given instruction that only champagne was to be served but one of the officers from the inspector generals staff requested red wine and an officer, not wanting to be rude, ordered that a bottle of red wine be brought to the table. When Cardigan saw the bottle he freaked out and started shouting, "BLACK BOTTLE!! BLACK BOTTLE!!! WHO DARES TO BRING A BLACK BOTTLE TO MY TABLE????!!!!"

Yup, the guy was a fucking nutcase. When the officer who had ordered the wine tried to explain Cardigan had him arrested. From that day on Cardigan harassed this officer so relentlessly that he ended up resigning from the cavalry. All these ridiculous shenanigans earned Cardigan an unpleasant reputation that spread even beyond the army. Leading up to the Crimean War there were demonstrations in the streets of London to try and get him removed from command. Once at a railway station he was surrounded by a crowd who booed and heckled him. In a theatre Cardigan had to be asked to leave because once the punters realised who was in their midst they would not stop booing, hissing and shouting 'BLACK BOTTLE!!' during the performance.

Public opinion was scandalised at the appointment of these three donkeys to command the expeditionary force to the Crimea. They were incompetent, unpopular, loathed by their subordinates and they hated each other.

Perfect. This mission just can't fail can it?

The battle of Balaclava was fought on October 25th 1854 and was the second major battle fought in the Crimean War. The British had scored an early victory against the Russians at the Battle of Alma and this had established a foothold on the Crimean Peninsula. The next step was to lay siege to the port city of Sebastopol which remained the main strategic objective of the allied forces. The battle of Balaclava was basically the Russian attempt to break the siege and relieve the city.

There were in fact three noteworthy engagements, not just the Charge of the Light Brigade. The other two were The Thin Red

Line, which was an abbreviated version of a description by the war correspondent William Russell ("a thin red streak topped with a line of steel"), The Charge of the Heavy Brigade, and of course, the Charge of the Light Brigade.

The battle started when Russians Cossacks attacked Turkish positions which had been poorly prepared, and they were quickly overrun. As the Turks retreated the Cossacks gave chase and hacked them to pieces. Watching this from their position on a nearby hill was the Light Brigade, and the men started getting restless wanting to intervene and help the routed Turks. But Raglan issued no orders, so the British Forces had to simply stay where they were. The Russians now controlled two of the ridges in the valley, but worse, they had captured several British guns that had been abandoned by the Turks. As an ex-artilleryman I can tell you that the idea of British guns falling into enemy hands is a very uncomfortable thing indeed. If you didn't know, (and if you haven't served in the artillery why would you), the artillery doesn't have flags as their colours, the guns *are* their colours, so guns being captured is the equivalent of the enemy capturing your unit flag. This success encouraged the Russians, and they moved on to attack a British encampment. But unfortunately for them whilst charging towards it they encountered a company of Scottish infantry and this was where the first legend, The Thin Red Line, was born. This phrase would soon become a general term for the British army succeeding where they really shouldn't have.

This line of Scottish Infantry looked like a small obstacle for the Russian cavalry but what the Russians didn't know was that the British had a secret weapon (apart from Scottish Infantry regiments that is). This weapon was the Enfield Pattern 1853 rifle-musket. This rifle was considerably more powerful and more accurate than anything else that had come before, and legend has it that a single volley ripped into the Russian cavalry and made them retreat. As they retreated Raglan ordered the

Heavy Brigade to pursue them. This didn't achieve much, and the Russian cavalry retreated behind some artillery guns.

This is where one of the theories starts about why the charge of the Light Brigade happened. This first theory is that the Light Brigade was keen to charge after the Cossacks who they thought we're not playing fairly when they cut down the retreating Turks. Also, they were hacked off that the Heavy Brigade and been given the job of chasing them and had not done much with the opportunity, so they were looking for an excuse to go after the Cossacks.

It was at this point that Raglan issued his famously vague order and it was carried to Lord Lucan by Captain Louis Nolan. It read 'Lord Raglan wishes the cavalry to advance rapidly to the front, follow the enemy, and try to prevent the enemy carrying away the guns. Troop Horse Artillery may accompany. French cavalry is on your left. Immediate.'

The problem with this order was that it was not clear which guns Raglan wanted the cavalry to attack. Did he mean recapture the guns that the Turks had abandoned, or was he referring to the well defended Russian battery that the Cossacks were hiding behind? This was a near suicidal objective as the attack would be straight at the muzzles of the guns at the end of the valley, whilst infantry on either side of the valley fired down into it. Lucan asked Nolan which guns he was referring to and Nolan waved his arm generally in the direction of the heavily defended Russian guns, not the captured British ones that Raglan meant. Nolan couldn't be questioned about his actions as he was killed shortly after. Lucan carried the order to his hated brother-in-law, Lord Cardigan. Their conversation approximated this:

Lucan to Cardigan - "You are to advance down the Valley with the Light Brigade, I will follow and support with the Heavy Brigade."

Cardigan to Lucan - "Certainly sir but allow me to point out to you that the Russians have a battery at the end of the valley to our front and riflemen on both sides of the valley."

Lucan to Cardigan - "I know it, but Lord Raglan will have it. We have no choice but to obey."

Of course they did have a choice. They could have asked for clarification or even disregarded the order as impractical as they could see they would be getting shot out from three sides. So why did they do it?

There are three different theories.

The first is the traditional one that Cardigan and Lucan were so incompetent they didn't realise how difficult the attack would be, and if they did, they did it anyway because they didn't want people to think they were sissies. This seems unlikely. As we saw from the conversation they had, Cardigan knew very well that charging that position was a bad idea.

The second theory is that, as mentioned above, the Light Brigade were so fired up that they deliberately misunderstood the order and went after the Cossacks anyway.

The third theory is that Lucan deliberately misinterpreted the order so that he could send his brother-in-law into a very dangerous situation, possibly one that would end with his death. This third theory is pretty speculative however, and there is only one piece of evidence to support it, but that piece of evidence is pretty damning. Lucan, despite the orders, didn't follow up with his Heavy Brigade.

Whatever the reason, the Light Brigade attacked the end of the valley whilst Russian artillery fired rapidly into their faces and infantry fire poured into their charge on both sides.

A small detail, but an important one to see into the minds of the people there, it is a historical fact that at no point did any person of any rank hesitate in this attack or raise any objections.

Incredibly, the Light Brigade actually got to the end of the valley, captured the guns, and gave the Cossacks some serious punishment. Unfortunately, the Russians immediately counter attacked and the Light Brigade had to withdraw. Yes, they had to ride back down the valley where they'd been shot to ribbons in the first place.

600 men had embarked on the charge. 110 were killed, 130 were wounded, and another 30 or so wounded and captured. 375 horses had also been killed or had to be mercy killed afterwards. And incredibly, unbelievably, Lord Cardigan got away without a scratch.

This disaster was later portrayed as a shining example of the willingness of the British military to engage against very strong enemy whatever the odds.

But some good did come out of the Crimean War. The army was reformed and purchases of commissions were stopped so people like Lucan and Cardigan could no longer buy their way into positions of command. The treatment of wounded soldiers was also revolutionised. Disease accounted for a huge number of the 250,000 casualties lost by each side and when news of the terrible conditions at the front reached the British public there was outrage. Famous nurses like Mary Seacole and Florence Nightingale made their way to the theatre of operations and changed forever how battlefield casualties were treated. Legend has it that Florence Nightingale met army bosses in London and invented the mathematical tool of pie charts to show the loss of human life to treatable infections and was turned down flat. Clever woman that she was, she pointed out that better treatment would mean the soldier could return to military duties and grudgingly, they allowed her to go.

The poet laureate, Lord Tennyson, saw a report about the charge in a newspaper and wrote a poem that became famous. (By the way, a league is about three and a half miles.)

Half a league, half a league,
Half a league onward.

All in the valley of Death
rode the six hundred.
"Forward, the Light Brigade!
Charge for the guns!" he said.
Into the valley of Death
Rode the six hundred.

"Forward, the Light Brigade!"
Was there a man dismayed?
Not though the soldier knew
Someone had blundered.
Theirs not to make reply,
Theirs not to reason why,
Theirs but to do and die.
Into the valley of Death
Rode the six hundred.

Cannon to right of them,
Cannon to left of them,
Cannon in front of them
Volleyed and thundered;
Stormed at with shot and shell,
Boldly they rode and well,
Into the jaws of Death,
Into the mouth of hell
Rode the six hundred.

Flashed all their sabres bare,
Flashed as they turned in air
Sabring the gunners there,
Charging an army, while
All the world wondered.
Plunged in the battery-smoke
Right through the line they broke;
Cossack and Russian

Reeled from the sabre stroke
Shattered and sundered.
Then they rode back, but not
Not the six hundred.

Cannon to right of them,
Cannon to left of them,
Cannon behind them
Volleyed and thundered;
Stormed at with shot and shell,
While horse and hero fell.
They that had fought so well
Came through the jaws of Death,
Back from the mouth of hell,
All that was left of them,
Left of six hundred.

When can their glory fade?
O the wild charge they made!
All the world wondered.
Honour the charge they made!
Honour the Light Brigade,
Noble six hundred!

Was there a man dismayed?.... Someone had blundered...
Theirs not to reason why, theirs but to do and die...
To be honest, poetry is not my thing, but this puts the hairs up on the back of my neck. And a century and a half after the event, it still resonates.
The poem was probably the most popular one of the Victorian age and was published in a pamphlet and immediately became a national hit. Copies of it even got as far as the soldiers still fighting in the Crimean War and by the end of the 1800s it was generally expected that any good school child would be able to recite the entire poem from memory. Had Tennyson not

written the poem it is unlikely that this obscure cavalry charge would have become the legend that it is. It has echoes of the famous stand by 300 Spartans at Thermopylae and doubling the number seems to double the bravery.

The war ended with the signing of the Treaty of Paris on 30 March 1856 which left Russia in a weaker position than when the war had started.

I will give the last word to the Canadian Military historian Dr. Lynette Nusbacher who was a lecturer in War Studies at Sandhurst Military Academy.

Interviewer - "Was there any good that came from The Charge of the Light Brigade?"

Dr. Nusbacher - "Actually, yes. It showed the world that the British soldier will do anything, *ANYTHING*. And this is a legacy that haunts Britain's enemies to this day."

Researched and written by Jonno DP

It's what you would expect from an RSM

All Regimental Sergeant Majors of Army Apprentice Colleges (AAC) were from Guards Regiments for many years and from January 1987 to January 1989 I, as a Welsh Guardsman, was the RSM of the AAC in Chepstow where young men, predominantly Royal Engineers with a small number of Royal Corps of Transport, spent two years training for their particular trade. There were three apprentice colleges with our Royal Engineers from Chepstow, Royal Signals from Harrogate and REME from Arborfield and every year a college would host a Triangular Games weekend when all three would compete against each other. However, the AAC Chepstow also competed against the Royal Navy apprentices from HMS Collingwood, home and away. As RSM I would naturally travel to said Colleges to support Chepstow Apprentices. When we visited HMS Collingwood, all Chepstow Warrant Officers and Senior Ranks were invited to use the Royal Navy WOs and POs Mess and the courtesy was reciprocated when HMS Collingwood visited Chepstow at a later date.

Back then (and maybe still now) the Navy didn't seem to have an appointment equivalent to an RSM. In their mess the senior WO1 was in effect the Mess President but he didn't seem to have the same, let's call it 'clout' as an army RSM. No disrespect is intended toward our excellent Royal Navy. When the navy WOs and POs arrived and had settled their apprentices into their accommodation, they were, naturally, invited to come to the WO's and Sergeants Mess. When they arrived I was there with several of my mess members to greet them. I was in No 2 Dress uniform as were my mess members, our visitors were wearing civilian attire. I addressed them with, "Hello Gentlemen welcome to the AAC Chepstow WOs and Sergeants Mess, I am Regimental Sergeant Major Everett.

Please mingle and get to know the mess members who will provide you with a drink from the bar."

In the Army you always address the RSM as 'Sir' and it is the RSMs prerogative whether to address ranks junior to him, by their forename (usually WO2's) or their rank or surname. I was circulating when one of our visitors approached me and offered his hand, something that wouldn't normally happen unless it was another WO1, but I gave him the courtesy and shook his hand. He introduced himself with "I'm Petty Officer John Smith." (After all these years the actual name escapes me). I responded with, "Hello John, please get yourself a drink at the bar." But being unfamiliar with army protocol he said, "What's your name?"

The temperature in the mess dropped a couple of degrees and I could see wide eyed army personnel caught in the headlights. How could they defuse this without offending their guests?

I was chewing the inside of my cheek with irritation, but I tried to be polite. "As I said when I introduced myself John, its RSM Everett."

The PO responded with, "Yes, I know. But what's your name?"

The amount of people who had noticed what was going on had grown and lots of Navy had realized there was a 'situation' as they realized they were conversing with soldiers who were no longer listening but staring at what looked like a problem.

Now chewing the inside of both cheeks, I said, "OK John, as I said, I'm the RSM." My mess members mouths were silent, but to a man their expressions were saying "Please don't...please don't..."

Well, he responded again with..... yes, you've guessed it. By this time many of my Mess members who were in earshot of this conversation had gone beyond disbelief and were quietly sniggering.

I needed to think of a way of defusing the situation and I could think pretty quickly in those days. I said, "John, do you know any bible stories?"

Surprised, he responded, "Not really."
"Well John," I said, "in the New Testament of the bible it is written that Jesus walked on the Sea of Galilee."
The mystified PO said, "Uhhh, Yes, I've heard of that."
"Well John. As an RSM, I walk two inches above it."
The penny dropped. "Ohhhhh! OK Sir, Can I get YOU a drink?"
With this sorted we had an interesting chat about the differences between army RSMs and WO1s, and a Mess President of Royal Navy WO and PO Messes. He must have passed the word to his colleagues from Collingwood because I didn't have to give another Bible reading during the weekend. We later both laughed about it, and I did allow him to buy me a drink.

RSM James Everett Welsh Guards

Friendship is being there when someone is feeling low and not being afraid to kick them.
Randy Milholland

Baby Sitting

When I was a WRAC in Berlin I met lots of interesting people. One of them was an American Captain called Katz who was well liked and friendly to everyone. He was a Cherokee Indian, but his wife didn't want anyone to know, he was so interesting to talk to. He asked me if I would babysit for him one Friday evening, and to make things easier I could stay there overnight. All was going well, the kids were in bed, and I had made myself comfortable on the sofa having found a film I wanted to watch but this stupid poodle appeared and started to shag my arm. I dragged it off me and tried to distract it but as soon as I let go it came back and started shagging my leg. Once again I removed it, but it got on the back of the settee, put its paws round my neck and started trying to shag the back of my head. Realising politely declining its offer wasn't going to work I picked it up by the scruff of its neck and put it in the cupboard under the sink and shut the door.
Perfect.
Then, the kids started. They were saying 'babysitter get me some cookies', 'get me a drink', 'wanna watch TV', do this do that do the other. This went on for ages and I was bloody shattered. I went to look at the bedroom I was going to sleep in, and the sheets had been slept in numerous times. I wasn't happy. I heard the key in the door, ran down and let the dog out of the cupboard before he found where his pooch had spent the last four hours.
The next morning we had pancakes, bacon and maple syrup which made up for it somewhat.

LCpl Linda Sykes (Rudkin)

A hairy situation

The RSM at 7 Signals Regiment, Andy Hickling, was not a happy chappie. On one Monday morning RSMs parade, out of the whole of 2 Squadron, only the SSM and one of the troop Staff Sergeants had both eyebrows and a decent haircut.
We had had a weekend of getting pissed and shaving eyebrows, partial eyebrows, complete heads and half heads. Even the OC, Digger Barnes, had two half-eyebrows and our Tech Staff Sergeant, Steve Meachin, had a Hitler moustache. It went on to Part 1 orders that shaving off someone else's body hair was now a prevalent offence and must stop immediately so we moved on to immac which had a much better shock value anyway. If you are unfamiliar with immac it basically burns off hair chemically and is activated by water. So you would wake up thinking, 'I was pissed last night, and I can't remember getting into to bed.' Panicked, you check your eyebrows and are reassured that they are still there. Then you'd have a shower and they would fall off! What fun!

Gaz Duffy, Royal Signals (1985-2010)

Busted!

I was born into the life of Pad Brat in BMH Rinteln in 1977. Funny, I still think of myself as a Brat even though we have lived in Rotherham as civvies for decades now. My memories of living in Germany and being part of army life are the happiest of my entire childhood. From being woken up at daft o'clock in the morning from a loud knock, for dad to go on exercise, to playing inside the tanks and four tonners. Also having an ID card with my name and photo on to get into John Buchan school made me feel very important! I remember soldiers standing at the school gates and patrolling the streets when we were on high alert. I always felt part of a large army family, and everyone looked out for each other, but I did somewhat spoil a Christmas one year.

My Dad, Dave 'Hovis' Brown, was in the RCT with 3 tank transporter Squadron in Antwerp Barracks and used to run the Corporals mess with my Mum, Joan.

Over Christmas 1983 (so I was about 6) we had a childrens party at the barracks and every Brat took it in turns to up to go and sit with Father Christmas, have a wide-eyed awestruck chat with him, receive a present, then leave in a trance like state feeling you were the most special kid in the world. When it got to my turn I went and sat with Father Christmas and my awe turned quickly into suspicion. Suspicion hardened into certainty, and this quickly turned into the level of outrage that only six-year-olds feel. I jumped off his lap and shouted a warning to the excited queue of kids, **"THAT'S NOT FATHER CHRISTMAS, THAT'S MY DAD!"**

This announcement silenced the entire room. Then the adults came to their senses, someone laughed, and I was quickly ushered off stage. I just couldn't understand peoples reactions. Some adults were laughing, some looked panicked and all the kids in the queue were now staring sceptically at 'Santa'. Why people weren't pleased that I had done this mystified me. No present BTW.

Shelly Brown. Asseburge Strasse, Paderborn, then Loseke strasse, Sennelager.

Out for a quiet drink

In total I spent eleven years in BAOR. Six of them as a pad brat in Monchengladbach as dad was a Rice Crispy Tester from 1976-1982. I wish mum and dad were still around, they had some toe curling stories. I joined the Scots Guards in 1987 and got posted to Hohne until 1993, but then I had to get back to real life when the Battalion got posted to Windsor. Public duties are a totally different monster but just as funny.
If you had a guard free weekend in Hohne you had the choice of Hamburg to the North or Hanover to the South and we were especially enthusiastic about these options at the end of the month when we all got paid and were therefore all rich. We finished at lunchtime on Fridays, so it was a quick shower, a change of clothes and a towel chucked in a bag, (the reason for this will become apparent shortly!) and off we went in Woodys (Kenny Woodhead Scots Guards) Nissan Micra.
One weekend we got to Hanover along with Vince Hartnol (Welsh Guard attached to 1SG), parked up and went straight off to the Bierkeller for glasses of weissbier the size of buckets with a handle on the side. Around 1800hrs we went off to the Hannen Fas via a bratty stand and had either a kiste (9 glasses) or a metre (15 glasses) of Hannen Alt which was old beer like a stout. I am sure you can imagine what the next mornings dump was like!
After a fair few hours in there it was off to the Rhure, which was a sort of night club with a big round door at the entrance. You would think that Guardsmen and Goths would not mix, but we had some of the best laughs in that grungy place with only long benches to sit on. By 0300hrs you would think that would be it, but no! Off to a nightclub in an old cinema, which I cannot remember the name of for the life of me, but by then the alcohol volume had to slow down so it was shorts by then. After a couple of hours of dodgy dancing we would fall out of

there around 0600hrs and go for a McDonalds. Bonus! McDonalds serve beer in Germany.

At 0800hrs off to the Irish bar that was just opening to have a couple of quiet beers or possibly some really strong coffee. Remember the bag? Well now we would go back to the car, grab the bag, off to the swimming baths, shit, shower, shave and fresh clothes, then guess what? We would go through it all again on Saturday. (Absolute muppets!)

On one particular weekend we could not park the car in the usual place, so we found another place which we thought was actually better, little did we know! By 2am on Sunday morning we were all absolutely shit faced and totally bolloxed, so we wandered back to the car for a kip. I was in the passenger seat, Woody in the drivers and Vince in the back. It was Autumn time so it started getting light around 7.30 ish. I remember being woken as it was quite noisy outside the car. It is hard to describe the environment at that moment. We stank of booze, the car reeked of farts (old and new), we all ponged a bit from the sweaty overenthusiastic dancing and we had taken our shoes off for comfort. I might be mistaken, but I seem to remember the condensation on the inside of the windows had a slightly brown tinge to it and was a bit sticky to the touch. We couldn't see a thing outside as all the windows were steamed up, so I slowly wound down the window to see what was going on. I quickly wound it back up and started pissing myself laughing which woke the other two muppets up. Someone yawned, scratched, concentrated for a moment on a squeaky fart and said, "What's up?" "Look outside." I said. They wound down their windows and instantly started pissing themselves laughing as well. Whilst we had been asleep the car park had emptied, and we were now right in the centre of (and apparently the biggest attraction of) a large flea market. Most of the Germans walked past having a chuckle but there was the odd one who raised an eyebrow and shook his head. We got

out of the car as casually as we could and straightened ourselves up stretching and yawning.
The smell of a bratwurst stand about fifty yards away wafted over, so we headed there for breakfast. We had to wait until 2pm for the market to clear enough so we could get the car out and drive back to Hohne.

Chris Martin (AKA The Gonz)

The boy who cried 'gook'

One day we were sent to do a site guard at Munster-Nord. It was around the time that loads of Vietnam films were being being released, Platoon, Full Metal Jacket and the like. For those that haven't done this site guard, it is guarding a nuclear missile site and you usually go there for 2 or 3 weeks. At this particular site, the QRF and soldiers not on actual duty were housed at an old school about 5 or 6 km away. Site guards are the most boring activity I have ever done as a soldier. Unlike a camp guard its weeks, not a day and nothing, **nothing**, ever happens. You get bored with reading, bored with eating, bored with board games, bored watching films. Even more boring is being on stag. One of our techs, Jock Hardie, was on stag standing in one of the sangars and was bored.
Bored, bored, bored.
Bored in the kind of way that only stagging on a site guard can do.
The night had worn on and Trivial Pursuit over the intercom had finished. Jock was staring out into the woods, bored, very bored! A thought came into his head that he thought would amuse everyone, and would alleviate the boredom, albeit briefly. Unknown to him it was also an idea that would get him busted and fined quite a bit of cash.
He picked up the phone that went direct to the American guard room, wound the handle and shouted, "There's gooks in the wire, gooks everywhere I tell you, they're going to overrun us!" Jock thought they'd see the funny side and that he'd get a bollocking, but he was wrong. The British and the American sense of humour often doesn't mesh, and the yanks defo didn't see the funny side this night.
I was the 2i/c of the QRF, sitting at the school and the crash-out alarm goes off, followed immediately by a call from the American guard room. "This is a NO DUFF, I say again NO DUFF.

Site being attacked, Quadrant blah (memory isn't that good!), GCP will assist en-route".

On the way to the site, the GCP (German Civil Police) kept traffic lights and junctions blocked to allow us free passage and one of the Bedford's even smacked a German civilians car – not stopping either. We got to the site and dropped as close as we could to where the 'breach' was, met up with the military working dogs and off we went to secure the section that had gooks all over it! Mid-winter at Munster-Nord, trying to keep some semblance of control and not getting bitten by the very excited dogs was not easy. (Everyone ended up being totally knackered the following day.) When we got there, Jock shouted out of the sangar, "How do you like your night off wankers??!!".

We knew then that this was all a load of shit and radioed into the command cell that there were NO intruders, or potential intruders. It was bad enough getting crashed out by the Yanks or the Squadron HQ, but it's even worse when it's one of your own. To make matters worse, when I did the headcount and ammo check one of the lads had lost a magazine of 20 rounds. It was decided we would look for it the following day, as we hadn't a cat in hell's chance of finding it at night. When we got back to the school, one of the lads found Jock's holdall and took a quiet shit in it. We found the magazine by the way.

Gaz Duffy, Royal Signals (1985-2010)

"No man is a man until he has been a soldier."
Louis de Bernières

Sleep safe lads

During the eighties I was with 51 Ord company at Barker Barracks in Paderborn. This Barracks had two big regiments in it, 3rd Royal Tank Regiment and 3rd Regiment Royal Horse Artillery and a few smaller units like mine. Similar they may sound, but they could not have been more different in their approach to all things army. There were two ways into camp after a night out, the main gate guarded by shiny 3 RHA blokes doing it all by the book and the back gate 'guarded' by 3 RTR. When the Bikini state went to red it seemed like half 3 RHA was on guard duty. At one point 3 RHA had 6 blokes on the gate, QRF riding about in land rovers and eight two-man foot patrols. The place was a fortress. Well, except for the back gate guarded by 3RTR. They had one scruffy bloke on the gate and he usually didn't bother checking your ID. Guess which one we used when we came back to camp!

Ian Dayus. 51 Ordnance Company.
(This is spot on true by the way. I was one of those poor bastards stagging on the 3RHA gate – Jonno DP.)

The Branding of The North Irish Horse

T'was several nights before Christmas, just over a year since I left the Squadron, and not a sober man could be found. The date was the 13th of December 2014 time - 20:15 hours according to the photographer of the incident, Corporal, now Sergeant, PM. (Only using initials as some of these people are still serving).

I was invited down to the yearly squadron Christmas party and when I arrived the lads and girls had already had their Christmas dinner at 13:00hours, minus the food fight because the SQMS was tired of cleaning mashed spuds from the ceiling. They were all very merry with several cans inside them already. I walked into the hall to find a few Sergeants finishing up the cleaning of the pots and pans and continued onto the JRC, hearing roars of laughter as I walked up the two flights of stairs. I was greeted by a naked Corporal 'CB' on a mountain bike at the top of the stairs. Ahhhh.... The traditional annual naked bike time trials around the top corridor. 'Easy!' I hear you say, but there are three fire doors and a five-step platform near the end.

I had left the Squadron in the June of 2013 after being promoted to Sergeant, so as protocol required, I rapped on the door of the JRC before entering. As I came through the door I could see that the usual games where being played. Amongst others there was naked wrestling, and one of my personal favourites, Human Beer Skittles. Just then I caught sight of a young trooper known as Dangerous Daniel (so named for his all-too-common dangerous fuckups) wearing the firemans steel helmet we kept behind the bar. This item was brought into play a few years ago for a certain Corporal PBs habit of fighting and turning up pissed on parade. Known as the Thrown Track award, it was given to the person that fucked up the most throughout the year.

As I walked into the JRC Trooper Dangerous had the helmet on and was being lined up for Human Beer Skittles. He was being held above the end of a long line of tables with four guys on his arms and legs swinging him back and forth giving it "One – TWO – THREEEEE!!! and sending him flying down the table to crash into a stack (a very large stack) of beer cans. I was told that they had put the helmet on because the first time they sent him down with no helmet he had split his head open. He didn't seem bothered either way to be honest, but when he removed the helmet there was a gash like a Czech porn video. After a few drinks with the guys I moved on to the Sergeants mess. A few of the guys where there but not a lot was happening, so I had a quick one and went off in search of the party animals. While walking back I heard a huge roar of drunken laugher coming from the officer's mess. Walking in I found the officers laughing at Corporal CB and Corporal PM who were standing by the open coal fire. Outside it was dark and cold so the fire was most welcoming. But what was less welcoming was the sight of these two corporals standing over (yes, over) the fire, bollock naked smoking cigars. I don't think I have ever laughed so much in all my life.

Either side of the fire there was two armchairs of the typical style you would find in an officer's mess, and a two-seater sofa facing the fire with Lieutenant Mr W sitting on one section of the seat smoking a pipe. I sat beside him and had a few drinks talking shit and laughing about old times and then Mr W produced a silver horses hoof snuff box with Christmas Cheer snuff within. We all tried it but made me sneeze like a motherfucker.

Then another wooden pipe was produced from Mr W's pocket, as I had asked him about the Christmas blend of tobacco he had and what it was like. Next minute I'm puffing away like I've smoked all my days, which I haven't.

From behind the bar came hurras and swear words as Lieutenant H was trying to open a champagne bottle with one

of the two polished ceremonial cavalry sabres that were kept over the bar. This is how the branding came about. The sabre was grabbed by Corporal PM who started waving it about like a drunken Zorro. Someone told him to return it to its place above the bar, but he said he wouldn't until he had branded one of the new officers. Things were already getting out of hand, one of the new young officers was wearing a Ralph Lauren tie worth 40 quid and after finding out how much he paid for it Corporal MR popped over his shoulder with a pair of scissors and cut it in half. Into the fire it went. Anyhow, we thought none of the new young officers would be stepping up to the mark when we heard someone yelling from behind the bar "DO ME! DO ME!!!" It was Lieutenant H. Up to this point Corporal PM had only been kidding about branding someone, but if he had a volunteer... well fuck it, why not? So the sabre went into the fire came out red hot and was slapped onto the ass of the lucky Lieutenant H before he came to his senses.
"YEEEEEEEEOOOOOWWWWWAAAAAAARGGGGGGHHHHHHHHHHHHHHHHHHHH!!!!" Never, and I mean never, had I seen someone move so quick. I was standing by the fire watching the shenanigans and I heard someone call, "Next!" To my amazement the OC replied, "Me next!" to which I said, "Fucken gimme that". Into the fire it went but this time when it came out it was glowing like a light bulb. With a merry swing of the blade, we were soon all treated once again to the smell of burning ass cheek.
"WOOOOAAAAAAAAAHHHHHHHHHHHHH!!!!!"
As he ran away to the bar a few meters away. I joked, "Here come back I haven't finished, there's the other cheek to do", I didn't think he would be silly enough to come back, by sure enough he did, and the sabre was back into the fire for a reheat then slapped onto the other side. The OC ran out of the mess, at the speed of a gazelle, across the corridor to the bar of the Sergeants Mess, jumped up onto the sink and blasted the cold water over a very sore bike rack. I thought that he would be

mad at me once the pain had sobered him up a bit and I should take this as my cue to leave, but no, we had quite a few more drinks before I set off home.

Sgt Achey 1997 to 2013. Long runs the fox 😉"

Name rank and number! Which one?

In 1971 I was 17 and a half and in search of adventure I joined the Scottish infantry division. During basic training, and four days before I was due to pass out, I had the bright idea of getting hammered and going absent. When I came back my troop sergeant was pleased to come to me and say "Right! You are backsquadded!" and as I didn't really fancy doing fucking Otterburn again I decided I wasn't happy with this so I fucked off again for seven months before going back to and handing myself in. While I was there I had the surprising experience of being interviewed by the SIB from Edinburgh Because I had a UVF badge on my jacket. They obviously thought I had some dodgy connections, but in reality I hadn't really known what it was, I just bought it and stuck it on my jacket because I liked the look of it. I'd never even been to Ireland.

Whilst awaiting the armys decision on what to do with me I was sent to the cookhouse to do fatigues. After two weeks of this my patience wore out and off I went again, but this time I did it properly and I stayed away until about 1974. By this time I was a bit bored of being a civvy so I went back to the recruitment office to sign up again. By now I was a bit older and wiser, so I didn't hand myself in as AWOL, I signed up with a fresh start. An RMP sergeant asked me if I had ever been in the army and I said no. It surprised me that there was no issue with this as I was using exactly the same name and other details as I used before but it didn't seem to get noticed. The one single difference in the information I gave was that I named my aunt as my next of kin rather than my dad.

So off I went to Woolwich to do my basic training and join the artillery. After basics I got sent to 16AD regiment that were stationed in Soest, West Germany

All went fine until 1975 when we were on tour in Northern Ireland. We were lining up a load of vehicles for a COs

inspection and I got crushed between two ten ton trucks. I was not in a good state and the army, of course, notified my next of kin. Naturally enough my auntie was surprised that the army had informed her and not my parents, as she had no idea that she was down as my next of kin. She told the entire family including my brother-in-law who hated my guts, and he tipped the army off that I was AWOL from years ago. The army took a keen interest in this information and I was invited to go and have a chat with an RMP sergeant called Daniels. As I walked into the room his first words to me were, "What's your number, rank and name son?"
Of course I said, "24327712 Lance Bombardier Black 16 Air Defence Regiment Staff."
"You lying little bastard it's 24248419 Private Black 1st Battalion Kings Own Scottish Borderers!!"
There wasn't any point in denying it so for the next hour I told him exactly what had happened and he couldn't believe what I was saying to him. He sat there listening to it amazed that I had got away with it, but at the end of it he in filled the statement, read it back to me, I signed it and he told me I could go. I asked him if I was under close arrest or open arrest and he said, "Well we're in Northern Ireland so you're not likely to do a fucking runner are you? So neither as far as I am concerned."
My troop commander grabbed me as soon as I was out of the interview and asked me what it was all about. I explained that I'd actually been absent from the army since 1972 and it was his turn to be amazed. One of my nicknames in the regiment was gatling gob and when word got out at what had happened the whole regiment was absolutely amazed that I'd managed to keep this quiet for so long. I phoned the Missus that evening and told her what had happened and she was shitting herself thinking I was going to get kicked out of the army, we had a baby on the way. I had had a good tour in NI, but the army has a long memory and a vindictive temperament and I couldn't see them just shrugging this one off. Time passed, the tour

ended and we went back to Kirton Linsey. One day out of the blue the battery sergeant major, a guy called Tom Pooley, called me into his office.

"Right Blackie!" he said, "You're on BCs orders."

"When?"

"Now. Take your beret off and come with me."

I was marched into the battery commander's office, Major Sulman RA, and after the formalities were over he said, "Bombardier, you are charged that in an interview with a member of the army recruiting office in 1974 you were asked if you had served in the army before, and you said no, knowing this to be untrue. How do you plead?"

"Guilty sir."

"Do you accept my award, or do you wish to go in front of the commanding officer?"

If you don't already know, when on orders it's usually a bad idea to go in front of the CO as he can inflict greater punishments than the BC, so you're usually better off cashing your chips in and just accepting what your battery commander is going to give you.

"I accept your award sir."

To my absolute disbelief he said, "Admonished Bombardier, march out."

If you don't know what that is, admonished means that you have been officially told off, but there's no further punishment. I had amazed the RMP Staff Sergeant, I had amazed my Troop Commander and I was told that I had amazed the entire regiment, but I can assure you that this amazed me more than all of them put together! But more was to come.

With the same feeling as you would get walking away unharmed from a spectacular plane crash I marched out. Traditionally the next part of this army rigmarole is the BSM taking you into his office where he would verbally lay into you (and sometimes offer you a physical version) for five or ten minutes, but not this time. After I marched out the battery

sergeant major stopped me and said cheerily, "Blackie, you've got five minutes to go and get properly dressed." By now I was so confused I wasn't sure which planet I was on, so I actually looked myself up and down, then impressed the BSM with the witty comeback, "Uh?"
"Blackie, what did the battery commander just call you?"
"He called me bombardier." I said.
"And what rank are you?"
"Lance bombardier, sir."
"Correct!" said the BSM. "The CO has decided to make you up to full screw for your fucking cheek!"
I don't know how true it is, but someone who should know told me much later that what I had done caused ripples that went all the way up to the CinC UKLF. Apparently they were bothered by several things. Firstly, I had managed to get away with it in the recruiting office, secondly, I had got away with it for a long time, and thirdly the security Services got involved because they didn't want unknown people joining in case they were pro IRA.
Apparently everybody above the regiment wanted to make an example of me, but the CO gave me a glowing report and kept me in. Again, I don't know if it's true or not but I was told that the CinC said to his advisers that if they kicked me out and I went to the papers and told them what happened they would all be up to their necks in shit. As far as I know I'm the only man ever in the British army with two army numbers. I was stunned that all they gave me admonished, I was expecting to be busted at least and probably going to nick as well. But in the end the only long term effect of the whole incident was they changed my army number back to the original one I got when I was seventeen.

Blackie 16 Air Defence Regiment Royal Artillery

A stupidity hat trick

When I was a S.T.A.B (stupid TA bastard) at the Prince William of Gloucester Barracks I did several... ummm... interesting things that may be worthy of volume 3 of We Were Cold Warriors.

The first one was just stupid. Several of us had a competition to see who could strip off naked, run across the parade ground to the other side and back the quickest. All of us got caught and we ended up spud bashing and waiting on.

The second one was cruel. We decided to shave Plug. He was a bit like sloth from the Goonies, sort of our regimental mascot and wouldn't hurt a fly, fuck knows why he joined the army. We all got back pissed after a night at the sticky carpet night club in Grantham and he got the short straw. We shaved everything including his eyebrows and he locked himself in a cupboard to sleep so we wouldn't do anything else to him. The next morning on parade he didn't turn up and a search and rescue mission was mounted. He was quickly found, still in the cupboard, still fast asleep. He was a good egg and didn't grass on us so got away with that one.

The third thing was bad luck. I was on my JCB FLRT course. We had to do an off road, obstacle course. Part of it was a steep incline leading to a sharp drop and then a steep incline again. To stop the Volvo travelling too fast, we had to deploy a retarder (an engine brake). I did, but it wouldn't engage. The Volvo went hurtling down the hill and smashed into the bottom. I was chucked out of my seat smacking my head on something hard. I must have knocked myself out as I don't remember what happened next, but and one of my oppos had to run after the still moving Volvo, jump in and switch it off and apply brakes. They were well-built those Volvos, even though the drive shaft was in bits and the sump was shredded, it kept

on going up that hill. What he did was brave, and I believe he got a commendation. Toast of the camp! I on the other hand, had trashed a £65,000 Volvo FLRT and was
put on a charge. Fortunately for me the charge was dropped in the end because the retarder was found to be faulty. You would think I had more sense, but I became a regular after that.

Driver Brimage 156 Regiment 1991-1994.

Hot stuff!

In 1985 I was stationed in the Netherlands on a NATO posting with several different nationalities as well as British Army and RAF personnel. We had just finished an exercise and had had a few post exercise drinks with the Colonel.
I was pretty knackered when I got home so I lay down on the sofa in front of the TV and fell asleep.
My wife who was doing some ironing directly behind me, stopped and went to change the TV channel. Whist she was doing this the phone, which was also directly behind me, rang which woke me up with a start. I reached behind me and scrabbled around for the receiver, found it, and put it to my ear. But as you may have guessed, it wasn't the telephone receiver, it was the hot iron!!
Needless to say, my colleagues gave me no mercy in their piss taking when they saw the burn marks on my face and for months afterwards if I went into a room where someone was ironing, they would, without fail, offer me the iron and say, "Rob! It's for you."
Probably the worst was when I went to Medical Centre on the Monday morning to get it looked at, and the MO was trying manfully, and failing completely, to stop himself from laughing!! I said to him "With all due respect sir, if you want to laugh, please do so. I won't be offended, and its nothing compared to what everyone else is doing!" And in case you were wondering, no, I didn't burn the other ear phoning for an ambulance.

Robert Sayers RAF

Officers on the ball!

We were out on the Ooloo on exercise and we got notified that we were under NBC attack and had to put on our Noddy suits and gas masks.
We put our suits on but because we were sealed in a 432 the masks were not needed, that is until the BC came calling so we put on our masks and opened the door. The Sergeant at the back, Dave Wilson, had broken an eye piece of his mask, prompting this conversation with our leader.
BC, "Who's that?"
Dave, "Sergeant Wilson sir."
BC, "Sergeant Wilson you have broken your mask." This is obviously the kind of perceptive brilliance that gets you through Sandhurst.
Dave, "Yes sir."
BC, "What would you do if this was the real thing?"
Well, die is the obvious answer. Or hold the BC at gunpoint and nick his. I mean what did he expect him to do? Leave the exercise, go back to Hildesheim and visit the Q stores? Maybe he could just close his eyes.
Another time in the middle of nowhere in Germany, the whole of shiny K battery had been parked up on the Sunday (the Germans liked a bit of peace on the Sunday, so exercises were paused for the day) and on Monday we all lined up ready to crack on. We were led down a road with our CP in the lead commanded by a Rupert (I forget his name now). After a bit he stops the entire column and addresses me on the intercom, "Bombardier Paterson, have you got your compass?"
"Yes sir." After all I was the CP ack and therefore pretty handy with all things navigation.
"Come here and check this sign, I think it's been moved."
I clambered down and stood next to a concrete post that was about 2 metres tall and 50 cm square. A good half a ton I

should think. If anyone had moved it, he was dressed in blue tights and had red pants on the outside. I made a theatrical show of checking it with my prismatic compass, returned to the front of the 432 and climbed up the front to look at the ruperts map jammed in the commanders hatch. From my perspective it is the right way up, so from his perspective its upside down. No wonder he thought the sign was wrong WE were going the wrong way. Rule 1 of map reading, taught to me in school, never mind the army, orientate the map with north on the map to the north on the ground. It's a bloody good job World War 3 never happened or he would have attacked France!

Colin Paterson G.S.M

Who shot the captain?

Now this was what I had joined for... a bit of fun! Although the WRAC was a non-combatant corps, we still had to have weapons training which was just so cool. The day had arrived and we were going to the firing ranges several miles away. We awoke very excited and couldn't wait to get to the yard. We all marched down to the armoury, were issued with, and signed for a sub-machine gun. We had previously been given instructions and a practical lesson on how to clean, load, and unload our weapons against the clock. By the time we received them, we felt like snipers.
As we boarded the MK (big truck), the morale amongst us was high. On the way, we stopped off for bacon and egg banjos (banjo being a bread roll) and doughnuts. It really was turning out to be a brilliant day. Perhaps what made my view of a good day in the army wasn't quite in keeping with what was expected... I took a rain check on the banjo, but the doughnuts were a different story. Whenever they appeared, it became competitive and I was the doughnut champ. It had to be sugar doughnuts filled with jam and you had to eat the entire thing without licking your lips. It may sound incredibly easy, but it was far more difficult than you can imagine. Try it and see! When there's sugar all over your face and jam up your nose, you get an overwhelming urge to lick your lips. This was the day I was to smash my record of two consecutive doughnuts by eating four without licking my lips once. I was a mess but, boy, they tasted good, and it was a great source of entertainment for the journey to the ranges. Hey, if you can't laugh at yourself then who can you laugh at? Anyway, I'm veering off course here.
We arrived at the firing range and the excitement was almost too much for us to bear despite our trepidation. There was a smell of cordite in the air, and we were champing at the bit to

be let loose with a weapon. The place was vast and very impressive, with about five acres of land divided up into different ranges. Although very quiet overall, the silence was randomly broken with rapid gun fire in the distance. Captain Jones (our troop captain) made sure very quickly that we were all in check by bellowing at us and getting us huddled around for a briefing. We were ready. The targets were at one end of the range, and we were at the other. What's the worst that could happen? Ah, shit happens to me. If anyone could spectacularly screw this up, then it would, of course, be me. The single-round firing went swimmingly, and I did some rather impressive shooting, if I say so myself. At the end of the session, we were told that, if we had any rounds left, we could switch our weapons onto automatic mode and fire at the target, obviously making sure it was clear to shoot. I had clearly not been listening — again — when the instructions were given because I was unaware the gun would handle differently when fired on automatic. I squeezed the trigger and the strangest thing happened. I seemed to lose control of my body. Instead of firing down the range, I was thrown back by the force of the weapon and lost my bearings. My position shifted and I appeared to have turned slightly to the left, still with my finger on the trigger. Oh boy, was the firing loud. After what seemed like an eternity, but in reality was probably only a few seconds, it all went deathly quiet. Had I gone deaf? I was shaking a little as the force of the shot had been a hell of a shock. I felt emotional and winded. Out of the silence, I could hear distant swearing and screaming. I turned to see who was making all the noise and I was suddenly very aware that it was directed at me. I didn't understand and everything was jumbled up. One minute I had been an extra in a James Bond movie with the single shot firing and the next minute the captain was screaming and swearing at me. I was dragged to my feet — the firing had put me on my ass — and frogmarched over to the captain who was bright red in the face and pointing to his boot.

I followed his gaze and couldn't see anything. He continued pointing, still swearing and shouting. I looked closer and there it was... the tiniest little nick in the leather of his left combat boot, just above the ankle area.

"You crazy bitch, you shot me! What the hell did I say about firing on automatic?" he screamed in a heavy Scouse accent. "I distinctly said you were to make sure the area was clear and safe. Are you stupid? Did you not see me?" He kept repeating himself over and over again. OK, OK, I heard you the first time. He was so angry he was spitting as he screamed at me. Dare I say he was overreacting a tad? Maybe not. I hadn't actually shot him, just his boot and, even then, it was just a nick. I don't know who was more frightened, me or him. I was going to point out I did check and the area I was aiming for had been very clear and safe, however, I hadn't banked on going slightly off course due to the impact of the weapon, but I held my tongue as now was clearly not the time for reasoned arguments. The journey back from the firing range was very loud as the girls kept repeating "You crazy bitch, you shot me!" followed by howls of laughter. Luckily for me, by the time we returned to base, he had just about seen the funny side of things and I wasn't placed on a charge. I never did that again!

Lorna McCann

This story appears in Lorna McCanns excellent book 'How not to be a soldier.'

While my coffee pot gently weeps

We had some really odd characters in 4ADSR (1ADSR after its renaming ceremony). Whilst there I got to know this young lad called George Harrison – real name – George Harrison, who was from Stoke on Trent and who had a biff-chit for his mental state.

At the time, I was a Workshop Sergeant and George was one of the troop lineys, so was a frequent visitor to the workshops to order spares, cable, etc. As he was a frequent visitor, I got to know him, and ended up quite liking him, despite him being a little 'mad' as it were. He used to say he loved coming in the workshops as we didn't treat him like shit. We always used to have a pot of coffee on the go, so George asked if he could join the coffee fund so that he could have fresh brewed coffee when he visited. I agreed and said, "Your first job is to go to the NAAFI. Here's 20 marks, grab some coffee, sugar and milk powder." Off George bimbles and about 20 minutes later, returns hands me the coffee, sugar, milk powder and the same 20 mark note I gave him before. "Here you go Sarge." says George.

Naturally I queried this.

"I just pull out my chit and tell 'em I'm mad and they always let me go no problem." Not that I took advantage, but from then on George was always the one sent to get supplies from the NAAFI.

One time George was walking up the road with his hands in his pockets when he was spotted by the RSM. The RSM gave the response which was typical of his rank. "Hands cold? what are you mooching around MY camp for?" ...etc.. etc. The RSM squares up to him and continues shouting when George doesn't take his hands out of his pockets. He carries on until he's red in the face and literally spitting all over George. George waited for him to inhale and said, "You know, I could batter you and get away with it you jock cunt, 'cos I'm fucking mental!" At which point he waves his biff-chit at him and slowly turns and walks away. The Rasman was apoplectic but didn't have a clue how to respond. I did, I pissed myself laughing!

Gaz Duffy, Royal Signals (1985-2010)

I have a cunning plan...

Easter leave 1983. Me and a mate we called Dave The Cardboard Box spent most of the leave at my parents house in Cirencester having a great time. As usual, squaddies being squaddies, we wanted as much leave as possible so we arranged everything so we would get back to Paderborn just a few hours before the parade at 8 0'Clock on Monday morning. Everything was as last minute as possible but timed to perfection. Train timetables, when to change, which platform, connections to the ferry, trains on the continent... the lot. The journey went exactly to plan, and we were congratulating ourselves on a slick bit of organisation until we reached Dortmund which was about an hour away from Paderborn. Unknown to us, but knownst to the Germans they, with their usual efficiency, change the train timetables at the same time each year (end of March) so everyone knows they need to take extra care with travel arrangements at that time of year. Well, almost everybody.
At 10.30 at night we were standing on a cold railway platform in Dortmund waiting for a train that was due now-ish. Unfortunately it was a train that no longer existed, having left at 9.30 ish. As it slowly sank in that we were waiting in vain we went off to find out what the score was. The score was that there was another train but it didn't leave until 6am. We did some quick calculations and figured we would get in to camp at about half past seven leaving us just enough time to get on parade for 8. Ok, no problem we thought!
We arrived at Paderborn bahnhof, jumped off the train before it stopped moving, ran to the taxi rank and jumped in telling the driver, "Panzer Kaserne, schnell!" What we didn't know, as we ran into the block at about 7:20, was that the battery, in all their glory, were lining up for PT, which started at 7.30am rather than 8. A few people saw us and smiled, but we knew no

one was gonna bubble us so we legged it toward the room thinking 'Shit this is close but we are *just* going to get away with it!'. But as we pelted into the block we ran straight into a PT clad BSM WO2 Geordie Cutter and skidded to a halt. True to his usual form all he said was, "I'll see you two outside my office when we get back.... I want to know why you are late." Ten extra duties for that one.

Dene Rose J Sidi Rezegh Battery 3RHA

You don't need a title to be a leader.
Anon

Fine dining in the DDR!

In December 1965, a colleague and I, serving with 13 Signal Regiment in West Germany were transferred to the Royal Signals detachment at RAF Gatow, Berlin. It was at the height of the Cold War and east-west relations were at a low point. We travelled via Bundesbahn to Brunswick and because of our security status, were escorted by RMP onto the British Military Train which ran daily through East Germany to Berlin. On boarding, we were instructed to read and comply with written instructions during the journey. 'No contact with anyone outside the train, no photography, no open windows, hats could be removed but otherwise formal military dress codes observed'.

An armed guard (RGJ) patrolled the train and after checking that all doors and windows were firmly secured we left Brunswick at 1630. Deep snow lay all around and it was bitterly cold. As we crossed the Inner German Border from West to East the countryside was plunged into darkness.

We stopped at Marienborn, the first East German station, as the German dining-car steward summoned us to dinner. We were sitting down just as the British Officer i/c train and a WO alighted and went to the Soviet Control Office with our ID cards and what looked like a bottle of whisky and carton of cigarettes. This was, no doubt, to smooth our passage. In the dining car the German steward, (crisp white jacket, red epaulettes), beckoned us forward and, presumably because we were in uniform and everyone else in mufti, showed us to a table at the centre of the dining car. The carriage interior was superb, each table adorned in spotless table linen, gleaming cutlery and glassware, the table lampshades bearing the HQ BAOR logo. We were a bit puzzled by this red carpet treatment and were waiting for the stewards boss to turn up and shout something in German along the lines of, "Not those two you bloody fool, the generals in carriage three." but we thought 'don't rock the boat when you are getting free stuff'.

A Russian soldier, fur hat, long greatcoat and Kalashnikov patrolled the frozen platform a few feet away. The steward arrived with the drinks trolley and offered an aperitif. Then came piping hot, beef soup and a basket of hot bread rolls, quite delicious. The main course quickly followed, fillet of white fish in a beurre blanc sauce, creamed potatoes and selection of fresh vegetables. A glass of beer, or a glass of wine was 15 pfennigs which was about sixpence.

As we were tucking in another train pulled to a halt alongside us, a pre-war East German train, shabby, overcrowded and clearly unheated. The frozen passengers stared at us in our beautiful carriage eating our sumptuous fare with hunger and acute jealousy, as did the Russian platform guard! The steward appeared with a bottle of chilled white wine and carefully poured a sample. He whispered to us,

"swirl.....sniff.....sip.....taste.....smile and nod. Gut, gut, sehr gut, look like you are enjoying it, Ivan is watching you."

We realised then that we were stooges in a propaganda stunt. Lowly soldiers being treated like royalty, for the benefit of those forced to live in the Soviet regime. We played our part well, ignoring the audience; we lingered, longingly over the desert trolley, apfel strudl, lemon tort, or schwartzwald gateau... then nodding when the silver coffee pot was offered. As we left Marienborn, the steward returned in a much brisker manner, "Fertig ihre essen bitte!" ('Finish your meals please.') The show, for today, was over!

Signalman D Boylan. Royal Signals, 1963-69

Who wants to be a gunner here?

In the last quarter of 1971 I was at 17 Training Regiment in Woolwich, a small 17-year-old kid, keen to do well and fairly confident as I had been a sergeant in the Army Cadets.
In our squad was a lad from Edinburgh, Gunner Oliver, who was less keen. In fact, he was a terrible recruit who didn't even want to be in the army, but his father had made him join up. I think he was trying to work his ticket, but it mustn't look like he was trying to get booted out for fear of his dad. One day we were to do map reading which made me feel good as I was taught to read maps in school, aged 12, and had plenty of practical experience for 3 years in the cadets.
We were told to fetch a map out of a box and the instructor spent an hour teaching us the basics, 6 figure grid references and all the rest of it with us following on our maps. Easy for me, I could already do all of this.
The instructor, a terrifying man known as Lance Bombardier John-Pierre, asked Oliver what was at grid 123456, "Ah dinnae ken bombardier."
"Why not Oliver?"
"Ah havenae got a map bombardier."
We shot horrified, amused glances at each other and it took all our self-control (and fear of the NCO) not to laugh.
Less than a fortnight later Oliver got his wish, but I'm sure that his father was not pleased.
One of the other guys in our squad was Jock Rea, (pronounced 'rear'). He was taken ill during training and sent to the Woolwich military hospital and some of the guys decided to visit him. It had not gone well. On their return they told us that they had gone into the hospital and politely approached the mean eyed receptionist.

"What do you want?" she asked with all the charm of a February morning in Moss Side.

"Gunner Rea?" (Say gunner Rear in your head and you will get it.)

A stony silence greeted this request before she informed them, "We don't have any cases of that here."

Colin Paterson G.S.M.

RAF Gatow, Berlin 1972 (The Goat)

My first overseas posting after three years in the Royal Air Force was to the popular RAF Gatow, which was located at the southwestern corner of Berlin, right alongside the infamous Berlin Wall. It just so happened that this posting came along with the label of being on Active Service, which meant that any charges issued against a serviceman started with the preamble, 'Whilst on Active Service being charged with the offence of………', which is important to this story.

I was a Junior Technician (J/T) within the Ground Radio Flight at RAF Gatow and working as a ground radar technician. This was a quite junior position, but it was an important job maintaining the radar and communication landing aids for the airfield. At the time that I was there, RAF Gatow must have been one of the quietest airfields in the Royal Air Force. There were a couple of two-seater Chipmunk aircraft which went up now and again, cruised over the wall and around Berlin, an interesting little trip when you could get aboard. There was also the trooper aircraft which arrived on Wednesday's, but apart from that, not a lot happened at RAF Gatow. We were there just in case the Russians did again what they did before and closed the road and rail corridors from West Germany into West Berlin. A lot of our time was spent finding other things to do in order to keep busy. We repaired private TV's, radios and even cars, and the camp had many bars and clubs, so the social life was always good fun.

As it happened, the Ground Radio Flight workshops were situated within the Air Traffic Control Tower, which was part of the main Station Headquarters (SHQ) building. This was not a normal situation, but I guess that the building simply carried on from its role as used by the Luftwaffe until they were kicked out at the end of WWII. The SHQ Building had a large secure fenced compound next to it containing a radar system and our Petroleum, Oil and Lubricants (POL) storage area.

So here I was, one afternoon pottering around in our radio workshop when another J/T by the name of Dennis Raite came rushing into the workshop asking for my help. Dennis drove a tatty old VW and needed to paint the rusty bits of his car (and there were a lot) with a type of paint called red lead that stopped further corrosion. The problem was that Dennis could not get access to the POL locker, as a ceremonial goat had been secured within the fenced compound, and it was a feisty beast, attacking anybody that dared enter its domain. The goat, along with its handler had been brought out from the UK to march at the head of the Royal Air Force Regiment and the British contingent of the Allied Forces, during the forthcoming Allied Forces parade, through the centre of Berlin.

The plan, or at least Dennis's plan, was that I would go into the fenced compound to distract the goat whilst he would get some red lead from our POL locker, simple. When we entered the compound the goat was elsewhere and didn't see us so the two of us undid the locker and started decanting a quantity of red lead into an empty coffee jar. We were so absorbed with this task that we had not kept an eye out for the goat who after a bit had spotted us.

The goat started his first attack run on Dennis from about twenty metres (the first of three) scoring a solid hit on his back. After the third successful charge by the goat Dennis started a strategic withdrawal that looked to me more like a panicked rout, legging it alongside the SHQ building, around the corner towards the access gate, closely followed by the deranged satan creature who seemed to have instantly developed an overwhelming and obsessive dislike for him. This left me alone to decant the red lead into the coffee jar which was a messy job on my own leaving me with red lead covering my hands. With adequate paint in the jar, it was now my turn to get out of the compound through the only gate. This was now guarded by the deranged goat glaring at Dennis who was now safe on other side. Carrying the jar of red lead, I managed to sneak up quite close to the gate which was guarded by the goat before the beast spotted me, I was hoping that Dennis would open the gate a little so that I would be able to make my dash to the gate and slip through before the goat attacked me. I was wrong, the goat went for me horns down and charged before I could get anywhere near the gate, but unlike Dennis who had a head start on the animal as it chased him out of the compound, the goat was positioned between me and the gate. Well, it charged, but as it wasn't that far away it didn't manage to pick up much speed, so I managed to grab a horn made slippery by the paint that was all over it whilst holding desperately on to an equally slippery and paint covered jar. After a bit of back and forth which shared the paint even more generously with the damned goat I finally succeeded in getting out of the compound gate. As I stood there panting and swearing at Dennis I comforted myself with the thought that it was all over and I didn't have any horn shaped holes in me.

I was right on the second thought, but wrong on the first. Unknown to us the whole venture had been seen by very entertained SHQ staff, who promptly reported it to the Military Police. Thats when it all started. We were picked up by the MPs quite quickly. We got the good guy/bad guy police treatment, with one of them offering me a coffee, and his mate shouting and bawling all sorts of abuse at me, for getting red lead on the horns of the Royal Air Force Regiments goat. This went on for some time and they were trying to get me to admit that I had attacked the goat with red paint on purpose and the whole sorry process was going nowhere. But of course the RAF has a long memory and the incident had secured me some powerful enemies at some quite high up places, primarily because the Military Police were peddling the story that I had buggered up the goat deliberately and that I was being awkward by continuing to claim self-defence.

The Royal Air Force hierarchy bided their time, and were able to throw the book at me some time later for another incident that I was involved in. For the moment though, I was in the clear as they presumably couldn't find anything to charge me with. (I had a mental picture of the clueless MPs checking the index of Queens Regulations under G for goat and S for self-defence but drawing a blank). So with the legendary vindictiveness that the MPs are well known for, they went full throttle after my mate Dennis. He was charged and found guilty of 'When on Active Duty, stealing a quantity of red lead paint from the Royal Air Force for his own personal use.' The angry goat didn't get off scot free either as the red lead couldn't be removed from its horns for fear of injuring it. As you can imagine, the goat handler was distraught, having to march his red horned goat in front of the massed crowds in Berlin. Apparently there are some pictures somewhere of the red horned goat marching at the front of the RAF Regiment on that parade.

This event kind of stayed with me throughout my entire Royal Air Force career of 23 years. In my time I did many detachments and postings throughout the UK and overseas, and I have found often found myself sitting in a foreign bar someplace and listening to someone talking about the goat incident. I believe that they must have been friends of the goat handler, as when discussed the dastardly goat painter had supposedly been thrown into jail or worse, after capture by the Military Police. For obvious reasons I always kept quiet.

The very last time that the goat incident came up (for me at least), was some fifteen years after the incident, and almost forgotten by myself. On promotion I was posted to RAF Binbrook in Lincolnshire and met my new boss, a Flight Lieutenant Simon Denser. We got talking and it turned out that Simon actually knew Dennis Raite, who had taken a commission and was now a Squadron Leader at RAF Buchan, a defence monitoring station located north of Aberdeen. Simon came up with the plan to call Dennis, and that Simon would pretend to be a Special Investigation Branch officer who had been tasked with investigating the death of an RAF goat, cause of death – lead poisoning.

"Squadron leader, our records suggest that you may be able to shed some light on this..." That kind of thing.

I was standing next to Simon when he made the call and all I could hear was a lot of shouting and screaming coming out of the earpiece.

When Dennis started bellowing, "WHO IS THIS??? WHO IS THIS?????" I took the phone from Simon and said, "Hi Dennis." I have a strong Edinburgh accent and Dennis immediately knew who it was.

Ken Macrae, Ex Royal Air Force

Explosion in the field!

During the 1960s, BAOR operated a communications base and a series of outstations and satellite units. It also operated a DF network with an outstation some five kilometres from the main unit. The site was in the middle of an asparagus field and access was gained via a rough track. Some distance from the radio cabin was a deep drop toilet in a small hut.

Early one morning shift someone from RHQ rang and asked the D/F operator to go and check if the deep drop toilet needed emptying. So during a break, he went to the privy, lifted the toilet seat and peered into the abyss. He realised it was too dark to see into the depths, so he took a piece of paper, lit it, and dropped it into the hole for illumination purposes. In his innocence, he knew nothing of methane gases, but he would find out shortly...

The burning paper floated slowly downwards until there was a huge rumbling Boooommmmm........ accompanied by a great ball of flame that soared majestically into the sky. Fortunately, the blast knocked him backwards out of the door so he missed most of the fireball, though he did get his eyebrows singed and his beret went flying.

He picked himself to see a German field worker, who had witnessed the incident, on his knees, clutching his belly, tears of laughter rolling down his face.

The siggy had an overdeveloped sense of dignity and attempted to walk nonchalantly back to the cabin as if nothing had happened giving the howling German a polite, "Guten morgen."

For weeks afterwards, when walking through camp, he was conscious of German civilian workers, nudging each other, nodding in his direction and saying delightedly, "Das ist er, Das ist er! (That's him, that's him.) Die Scheissen-haus Kommando!"

To be fair to him, he did get over it and told me this story after an evening of revelry in the NAAFI bar.
No names, no pack-drill.

Sig Boylan, Royal Signals 1963-67

Kilimanjaro days

I had ended my stint as Chief Clerk of 15th Signal Regiment in Aden and had time before my next posting was available. I had seen a request for volunteer instructors to spend a month in Kenya teaching at the Outward-Bound school on the slopes of Mount Kilimanjaro and it sounded like a great adventure, so I applied.

So it was, a few weeks later I found myself joining a bus load of young African students, some of them English lads who lived in Africa, for the ten hour trip to the village of Loitokitok over some very rough dirt roads.

The school was a few miles from Loitokitok at an altitude of about 8,000 feet and consisted of several huts each accommodating 8 students. There was also a cookhouse, instructors accommodation/canteen, sand volleyball court, assault course style training area and a swimming pool.

The general idea was to get every student fit and capable of making it to Kibo, the summit of the 19,300 foot high Mount Kilimanjaro, the highest mountain in Africa. We had a daily fitness routine, competitive assault course teamwork and almost continuous volleyball games between huts. As an instructor I was expected to be fit enough to not only take part but also to teach the routines. My military experience and mindset helped here, I really enjoyed the physical aspect of it all, so different from my signals communications skills.

As the school was funded mainly by the African government it was always short of cash and the cookhouse grub was cheap, poorly cooked and very basic. Thus, for almost the whole duration of my time there I survived on chocolate bars, fruit and good bottled beer. Occasionally we would nip into the village in the Land Rover and get decent grub from the village store.

As navigation was part of the course we took the teams on long treks through the Masai Mara and in the process of hacking through bush and elephant grass a wait-a-bit branch whipped back on me and put a two inch thorn through my lip. The students learned some military slang that day!!

I palled up with another VSO instructor, a great chap called Paul, a six foot Welshman, who had once trialled for Wales rugby.

One day the African students were free to trek into Loitokitok so Paul and I took the Landrover and drove into the Masai Mara for another look round and hopefully photograph some of the big game that lived there. We met some Kenyan hunters who had just shot and skinned a buffalo for the meat (very gory) and later we came across a large pool with a group of hippos grunting contentedly. We dismounted from the land rover and Paul tried getting some photos. The problem was that they were just bumps in the water and it wouldn't make a very impressive photo so we thought we would gee them up a bit so he could get a more impressive snap. We shouted and waved our arms, but they ignored us.

After repeatedly trying this we had seen very little, certainly not enough to make a decent photo, then one of us had a brilliant idea. Let's attract their attention by chucking sticks! We gathered some up and started throwing them at the now VERY interested hippos. After a bit one of the beasts decided we were persona non grata and made a series of plunges across the pond towards us, jaws apart! It might be surprising for some people to learn, and this is common knowledge out there, hippos are regarded as one of the most dangerous animals in Africa. Bearing this is mind, Paul stowed his camera whilst demonstrating his running-whilst-panicking ability and we swiftly headed for separate nearby trees as the angry hippo charged to the pool edge, emerged and slowly walked towards us making angry snorting noises. We sat up there, uncomfortable but safe and hoped the hippo would get bored before it got dark. Fortunately it did after about half an hour and ambled back to the pool and its pals. By the way, tree ants are also very unfriendly, but I still have a photo of the hippo charging!

An angry hippo coming for us.

Another day I was i/c a patrol doing a navigation exercise on foot in the Masai Mara which, at that time, was scheduled as a 'Shooting Block' which meant big game could be hunted if you had the appropriate licenses which is why the animals were hard to find, unlike in the touristy areas. Due to the minerals present in the local rocks compasses were often unreliable and the patrol had to learn to navigate point to point using line of sight.
One day the students had to find a certain 700 foot high rock outcrop some ten miles distant where they would be taught various abseiling methods. Of course they got lost, and we walked into a British white hunters camp by a river. The hunter had an American army general on safari with him who had shot a rare black-maned lion that day. I asked to see it and the

tracker brought a stinking bundle of skin and unrolled it. I was unimpressed. I would much rather have seen it strolling along in its natural glory. The general had also shot an impala that day and the camp cook gave us a nice chunk of steak to grill on our campfire. Whilst we were there the General showed me his hugely expensive collection of game rifles and I must admit they handled unlike any normal rifle. They were hand crafted and almost alive, if you could say that about a weapon designed to kill.

That night we camped in our bashas down river, feasted on the impala and slept well. In the morning I went back upstream to thank the hunter for his courtesy and the general for our impala treat, and the hunter asked me where I had camped that night. When I described the spot he smiled and asked if I had heard any low growls during the night. A bit surprised I said we all had, we just thought it was normal Masai night sounds. At this he fell about laughing. He then told me that he had lodged a carcass in the trees at this location to attract leopards as the American general was after another trophy. The fact that we also had a dog with us made him laugh even more – apparently leopards love dog meat!!

I invited the hunter, Dave, to the Outward-Bound camp at Loitokitok where he gave an interesting talk on his life as a white hunter - he even had claw scar marks on his back to prove his fascinating tales! His tented safari camp had been luxurious and cost $2000 per day and remember this was in 1966!

I loved Kenya, but sadly never made it back there. Perhaps with political situation there I wouldn't like it if I did!

John R. Royal Signals

Fire in the hole

I'm sure most of you have clenched a flaming rolled newspaper between your cheeks and danced. In this tale it had a different meaning. We were on exercise and for some reason weren't allowed to kip in our wagons as normal, so we had cammed up a 9 by 9 tent under the trees and were sleeping in there. The aircraft had been serviced and we all retired to the tent for some kip when some bright spark said, "Have ever set fire to your farts?"

He then promptly dropped his trousers and let one rip with a lighter between his legs, the tent was filled with an eerie blue light much to everyone's amusement. After a while one of our tent dwellers who I will call Shuggy piped up and said, "I've got one building!"

He unzipped his maggot, stuck his legs in the air and let it go. Wooosh!! There was a long blue flame thrower but with a lingering yellow afterglow. This was followed by a loud squeal and a shout, "MY ARSE IS ON FIRE!!!" This announcement was followed by roars of laughter and the smell of burnt hair. Unbeknown to us, in the darkness, Shuggy had dropped his pants as well as his trousers and had set fire to his pubes and was slapping them to put the flames out. He was definitely walking funny the next day.

Ian Payne (REME Aviation)

My holiday snaps

Who doesn't like leaving soggy England and going somewhere warm? Well, not if its Kuwait just before we attack Iraq and you haven't been issued the right kit. But here some of my pics to show you what a lovely time we had.
We were sent out there to drive DROPS trucks (Demountable Rack Offload-Pickup System). These are multi axled rigid trucks that are used for transporting up to fifteen tons of kit, especially ammo, and dropping it off next to an artillery gun or whatever needs it.

Shortly after this photo was taken we reloaded with shells for AS90 artillery guns and headed to 7 regiment Royal Horse Artillery. Much to our surprise, rather than dropping the ammo and moving on to the next job we were told to dig in.
"The war is starting tonight, so dig in."

"But sir... our orders are to drop and return."
"Nope, dig in."
"But sir, we're still in green kit not desert cam, we have no plates in our body armour and we have no rounds in our magazines"
Never believe a bloody word of it if the army ever tells you it looks after its soldiers, later that night we crossed the border. To be fair though, they had addressed some of our concerns. We still wore green kit that stood out like the balls on a bulldog against the desert sand, we still had no plates in our body armour, but we were given five rounds for our rifles from their QM. Each! Oooh! Lucky!!
In total darkness and with convoy lights removed we crossed into Iraq.
After a while we heard something up ahead. It sounded like a group of people. And.... is that music?
We advanced carefully on the position and challenged it. It turned out to be four US marines in a humvee, ghetto blaster on the hood smoking weed.
"Hey maaaan." they greeted us, "The wars started, fuckin hey."
Yeah, we crept up on you and nearly wiped you out.

We weren't always delivering ammo, sometimes we were delivering water. One day I was driving the truck above delivering water to all the camps. After I had emptied out the water, leaving it bone dry, the piece of crap burst into flames. I grabbed a fire extinguisher and triggered it in the direction of the fire. A tiny little puff of dust emerged and that was it. Shovels at the ready.

This was my mascot on Telic 1. Moments after this photo was taken we were given five minutes notice to move. This was a problem though. I was gasping for a brew and the water wasn't hot yet.
No problem.

Using the ingenuity the army is famous for I was balancing the BV (boiling vessel) on my lap brewing up as we set off. Unfortunately for me, my Troop Commander (female and rather hot) dashed out of the command post to halt us. Faced with the choice of running her over or slamming on the brakes I chose the latter and the BV emptied itself onto my lap. Panicking that I would have boiled balls and spend the rest of my life speaking in a high pitched voice I leapt out of the cab and stripped off all the wet clothing as soon as I hit the ground. I then stood there wafting the wedding tackle and swearing, as you do when you've just been scared shitless. When I had calmed down a smidge I realised she was still stood there looking at me. My lap and balls had blistered like mad and forever after she would greet me with, "How's your blue monster this morning private Glover?"

I think this photo speaks for itself. We had long periods with not much to do and a bored squaddie is a dangerous creature.

Leigh Glover

"The soldier's main enemy is not the opposing soldier, but his own commander."
Ramman Kenoun

Who killed Bambi?

There was this time on R and R in Batus in 1987. Karl Britton, Alec Downie, me, and a couple of others decided to hire a car and do a road trip to Saskatoon, Saskatchewan. Alec sorted the car and our jaws dropped open when he turned up on the camp with this massive Chevrolet Impala.... it was huge and shining silver in the sun. It was like new with not a mark on it! There were three of us with driving licenses and I couldn't wait for it to be my go! When my turn to drive came, I leapt enthusiastically into the driving seat! It was an automatic, so really easy to drive and I was absolutely loving it when out of nowhere a fuckoff great moose appeared out of the woods and started running alongside.
"Fuck me!" said someone. "It's Bambi!"
The great stupid creature just kept galloping along about 20 metres away from our shiny new chevvy. (Maybe we shouldn't have got an impala, they could be related.) Alec and Karl both had a driving licence longer than me and encouraged me to carry on, but drive slowly, which I did. Bambi had started off some distance from us, but the gap between the woods and the road started to narrow drastically, leaving him only feet away from us, towering above the car.
Then a lot of things happened quickly. Bambi bolted, ran in front of the Impala and stopped. I slammed the brakes on, but not quick enough. Crunch!!!
Bollocks!
Bambi was big, but so was the chevvy, so we left him a large pile of unmoving hooves and fur at the side of the road. Not that we could have shifted him if we had wanted to.
I can still remember watching Alec from a distance, dropping the car off on a dark rainy evening, handing everything over and

legging it. It wasn't quite so shiny and new as when we got it. We'd got away with it but forever after Alec always reminded me of that day by singing the Sex Pistols song, 'Who killed Bambi?'

Dene Rose J Sidi Rezegh Battery 3RHA

Interesting Military Stuff # 4.
Operation Algeciras, the Argentinian plan to attack Gibraltar.

When the Argentinians invaded the Falklands in 1982 they fervently hoped the British would protest but stop short of military action. They were very nearly right, and had they waited just a little longer the British ability to respond would have been severely reduced. The British military in general, and the Royal Navy in particular was about to be downsized which would probably have made a viable response by Britain impossible. This decision to reduce the size of Britains military was, and is, heavily criticised, but to be fair to the people running the country at the time Britain was in a seriously dodgy economic position and we simply didn't have much money. This then, begs the question of why the Argentinians did it. Argentinian historians have tended to paint the conflict as plucky little Argentina standing up to the might of Britain knowing that once the juggernaut of the British military started moving the outcome was a foregone conclusion, but this was not the case. In actual fact the Argentinian government was a dictatorship that was becoming increasingly unpopular due to civil rights abuses and an economic crisis so its leader, a man called Leopoldo Galteiri ordered his military to invade the Falklands knowing that the tiny British garrison would be overwhelmed and that this victory would lead to a sharp increase in his popularity. He knew it was a gamble, but he was popular in America as he was seen by the Reagan administration as anti-communist and had been helping the US with its clandestine operations in South America. He hoped that America would support him and pressurise the British to not respond militarily. He also hoped that the British would consider the operation too risky. He was wrong on both counts, but not by much.

Once it became obvious that the British were tooling up and heading south mob handed, some people with shitty underpants in Buenos Aires started looking about for something to make the situation less difficult.

The head of the Argentine Navy, Admiral Jorge Anaya, suggested that if the British military was attacked in Europe they would keep some forces there rather than send them to the Falklands, thus reducing what the freezing conscripts entrenched around Port Stanley would have to deal with. At first Anaya considered an attack in Britain itself, but this idea was dropped when they realised that a group of swarthy men with Spanish accents asking the way to the naval base in Portsmouth would be noticed by the locals. In the end the best bet was considered to be an attack on a Royal Navy ship in Gibraltar which, due to its proximity to Spain, had obvious advantages in terms of language and the appearance of the agents sent.

The broad outline agreed was that divers would cross from Algeciras to Gibraltar under cover of darkness, lay limpet mines with timers, and come back. Algeciras was chosen as the launch point as it was on the other side of the bay a mere seven miles away from Gibraltar.

Anaya remained in overall command of the operation and Admiral Girling was given responsibility for personnel selection and detailed planning. He sent two groups, one to observe, and the other to actually plant the mines.

The man leading the team in Algeciras was Héctor Rosales, a spy and former naval officer. The mines would be planted by, and I am not making this up, three former terrorists from the Peronist guerrilla group. It's surprising they agreed to work for the Argentine government actually, as their organisation had been blowing things up in Argentina for years, and the Junta (the Argentine government) had naturally enough come after them with all the tools that a dictatorship has at its disposal. The leader of the group tasked with laying the mines was Máximo Nicoletti, a diver and expert in underwater explosives. His father had served in the Italian Navy during World War Two as an underwater demolition expert and had started a diving business after the war. In the 1970's Nicoletti had joined the Peronist terrorist group and had carried out several terror acts including killing a police chief and his wife by blowing up the police chiefs yacht. He also sank a destroyer, the ARA Santísima Trinidad, that was under construction in Buenos Aires.

But before the decade was out Nicoletti was arrested by the Argentine version of the Gestapo the 'Grupo de Tareas' and taken to the Navy Mechanics School, which was a cover for a government interrogation and torture centre. It's worth mentioning here that this place was nasty, even by the standards of the day. During the so called 'Dirty War' that was happening in Argentina at the time, about 5,000 prisoners went into such centres and about 150 lived to tell the tale. One of the favoured ways of disposing of the bodies was to throw them out of the back of a Hercules transport aircraft when over the Atlantic. I say bodies, but mostly the victims were still alive when they were thrown out.

Anyway, Nicoletti escaped this fate by cooperating with the authorities and dobbing all his mates in. His expertise as an explosives expert was recognised and he was told to carry out terrorist attacks against Chile because relations between Argentina and Chile were poor due to a territorial dispute. These attacks didn't happen as the two countries reached a diplomatic settlement, so he was sent to Venezuela as a spy, but he was caught and deported back to Argentina.

The other two divers that would help lay mines in Gibraltar had both worked with Nicoletti before in acts of terrorism, Antonio Latorre and another whose identity has never been established, but went by the name Marciano.

The group was told that in the event of their capture Argentina would deny all knowledge and they were to say that they were patriotic Argentinians acting alone. Furthermore, they were instructed not to do anything that would annoy Spain and to not actually lay the mines until ordered to do so by Anaya. To maintain the story that they were not acting for the government Italian limpet mines were shipped to Spain in the diplomatic bag.

But this operation was not going to be as easy as it sounded. At that time the Spanish government had serious difficulties with several terrorist groups and was worried about those groups using the 1982 world cup (which was being held in Spain) as a cover, so the police requested the public to be vigilant and report any suspicious activity, especially in the travel industry. The team were issued false Argentine passports made by another ex-terrorist colleague of Nicolettis and were marked with false earlier entry stamps to Spain.

On the 24th of April 1982 Latorre and Nicoletti flew to Paris where Latorres passport raised suspicions, but they were allowed to continue. They crossed the French/Spanish border without problems and travelled to Madrid where they met the other two, Rosales and Marciano, and then on to the office of the Argentine Naval Attache to pick up the mines.

Whilst they were in Spain they communicated daily by telephone with the Argentine Embassy in Madrid, who would pass the messages back to Buenos Aires. When they moved towards Algeciras they went in three cars with Nicoletti in the lead and the other two ten minutes apart. They had no way to communicate (this was long before mobile phones were common) so the plan was if Nicoletti saw a police checkpoint he would turn around and warn the others. This was crucial, because if the police searched them the military scuba gear would be difficult to explain away, but that was nothing compared to finding a good excuse for a boot full of Italian limpet mines. At one point Nicoletti encountered a police roadblock and did a U turn to go back and warn the others. Unfortunately, they didn't see him and drove on past him towards the roadblock. When they too saw the roadblock they also did a U turn and got away without the Spanish police noticing. (Good stagging guys, sharp as a knife that roadblock.) Whilst in Algeciras they stayed in separate hotels, moved frequently and always paid in cash. They also frequently changed the hire cars that they were using. Now this sounds like good practice when you are reading a novel but stop and think about it. Who goes on holiday alone and always pays in cash? Their car changing activities were also noticed by the limited number of rental companies in town.

The team bought a telescope and watched the comings and goings out of Gibraltar. There wasn't much security in evidence, the two sentry posts were unmanned and there was only one small vessel guarding the port.

The first time they considered attacking was when a British minesweeper entered the port, but after checking with Admiral Anaya in Buenos Aires it was considered not big enough. A few days later, and I find this to be almost unbelievable considering the brief was not to annoy or embarrass Spain, Nicoletti suggested attacking a large oil tanker. They quite fancied this one as it would have the added advantage of blocking Gibraltar harbour. Had they attacked, it could have covered the coast with oil (and the tanker wasn't even British). Unsurprisingly Anaya gave that one a 'No' as well.

The hotel changing, car changing and endless reconnaissance went on for weeks which strikes me as bonkers, (and James Bond I ain't) as the attack only needed to be symbolic to create worry about further attacks. And the further south the task force went, the less likely parts of it would be pulled back to defend Gib.

Then a high value target, HMS Ariadne, arrived. Permission was sought for an attack, but again but a reluctant Admiral Anaya refused as the president of Peru had suggested a peace plan and it could be undermined by a successful attack. Later that same day the Argentine cruiser General Belgrano was sent to the bottom by the British submarine HMS Conqueror, the Argentine government seriously got the hump, and Nicoletti was ordered to attack as soon as possible.

The next day the dithering finally caught up with them. Two of the team went to the car rental to extend the hire for another week, but the owner, Manuel Rojas had become suspicious. I would have been too, remember the police were asking people to keep an eye out for suspicious activity especially in the tourism industry. The person renting cars always had car keys on him from other rental agencies, he always paid cash in US dollars, never came in when he said he would and kept extending rentals or bringing them back and renting another later. If I was *trying* to look suspicious I would have done all this, and I can't think of anything else.

Rojas had told the police about these activities, and they turned up and arrested the two men. The police then went and arrested the other two who, despite explicit orders telling them not to, soon told the police that they were Argentine agents. The arrests were kept secret and the Spanish government decided to quietly expel the four men. They were flown to Madrid, had their passports returned (which the Spanish now knew to be false) and were then flown to the Canary Islands with a police escort. In the Canary Islands they were put onto a plane for Argentina.

As a Brit it's easy to be angry with the Spaniards for quietly letting the men go, after all Spain had just joined NATO. But the Spanish have deep political and cultural ties with South America and they were trying to not piss anyone off. Had Britain found itself in a similar position with say, New Zealanders up to no good, would we have prosecuted them? Probably not.

So did they come close to success? I think the answer has to be no. Firstly it seems that the British knew what was happening in

Algeciras because they were intercepting communications between Argentinas embassy in Madrid and Buenos Aires. (This now makes the timing of the mens arrest look suspiciously convenient.) Had they not been arrested at the car hire office the British would have tipped off the local police and had them nicked on the beach.

Secondly, if the British knew an attack was imminent it would have been countered at Gibraltar.

Thirdly, the aim of the operation was to get the British to pull units back from the South Atlantic to defend European locations and I can't see a reaction to an attack like this being warships in a port. Doubling the guard, more harbour patrols etc yes, but I don't see a frigate in a harbour being much use to defend against terrorist attacks.

And finally, the British focus was now on the shooting war in the Falklands and that would probably have been the last place the British government would have taken assets from.

Researched and written by Jonno DP

Life with the TA

In 1971 two of us were volunteered to go to Hameln with a 30-ton low loader and two D6 bulldozers, which we thought sounded like a cushy number. Little did we know that it would be the detail from hell working with the TA.
Three TA units from Yorkshire were getting two weeks annual camp in Germany and would be supported by us two regulars. The first two of the units were easy to deal with and we got through it fine, but the Sheffield lot led by Captain Bankmanager (I forget his name, but he acted like a puffed up bank manager) gave us two weeks of pain.
I will pick out three occasions which will prove that some Saturday and Sunday soldiers did not take to regulars, well their officer certainly didn't anyway.
The first occasion was during the mine laying training for the TA lads. Anyone who has endured one of these will know all about them. You have a dozer (me), a 4 tonner and the mine layer which was basically a plough digging a hole into which said mines were dropped (primed of course). I mentioned to Captain Bankmanager that it would be best if I drove my D6 just in front of the 4 tonner and if it got stuck, I could pull it out. He of course wanted it done properly. Which meant I had to secure my D6 to the 4 tonner with a very thin pin. I explained that we would run out of pins as it never worked properly. Half a dozen broken pins later he came around to my way of thinking and we did it how I suggested it in the first place. Score one to the regulars. Unfortunately, the Captain did not like being wrong and he made me to pay for it later.
The second interesting incident was when they did explosives. We parked the low loader up at what we thought was a safe distance from the danger area and sat in the cab. I would have the job of filling in the small holes after they had finished and therefore had a few hours to wait. Unfortunately, we didn't

allow for their lax attitude to safety and common sense. After a few hours of relaxation, we heard the warning shouted and as we glanced out of the wing mirrors we saw huge great clods of earth travelling fast in our direction. A split second later they whacked into the cab making several dents. This was followed by a stream of abuse from my mate, the majority of which started with the letter with F or C and were directed at great volume towards Captain Bankmanager.

We emerged from the cab to look over the damage and despite having a fair bit of Germany on the low loader and dozers, little real damage had been done. I reported to the captain with my dozer and he said the holes might be larger than at first thought (yeah, we noticed that), but he was sure I could manage. I asked the all-important question, "Has the area had been made safe?" (In other words has he checked that there wasn't some undetonated explosive still in a hole).

He said that all the explosives had fired, implying that he didn't need to check.

I pushed on, "Sir, you have not physically checked for remaining explosive, but you want me to drive a bulldozer over it?"

His reply was hard to believe. "You regulars reckon you know everything, so get on with it!"

What should have taken an hour would now take me three as what should have been small holes were craters. After the TA chaps had gone off for their tea and well-earned break (not), I commenced my task, which included extricating myself from large holes on several occasions as my dozer kept sinking into the softened soil. The one plus was that all the explosives had gone off or I wouldn't be writing this.

I was determined to get revenge and the opportunity came sooner than expected.

Captain Bankmanager and his company were overnighting at the back of the Bridging camp at Hameln. Somehow I got roped in to stay with them instead of returning to my comfy bed in the barracks, only a short distance away. As you can imagine, I was not a happy Sapper and when the evening 'stand-to' was called, I found a nice tree to hide behind. The captain had obviously not read the POM (Plant Operator Mechanics) bible which basically said that we have infantry to do all of that. After my 30 minutes relaxing behind said tree we 'stood down'.

Then Captain Bankmanager decided that as some high-ranking officer would be dining with him that night some ass kissing was in order and it would look good to have a regular soldier on guard duty. Half an hour before the Brigadiers arrival I got my orders. On no account was I to hold up the Brigadier, and I was to escort him straight to the Officers Mess tent. What happened is probably the closest I ever got to being Court Martialled.

Unfortunately for the dear old captain my first employment when arriving in BAOR was an eight-month stint on the Regimental Police. His guest would not get past me unchallenged whatever rank he was.

The large black staff car made its way at a stately pace through the wood towards us and I was ready for it. I went for it with the SMG pointed towards said staff car and, "Halt who goes there?" thundered out. It certainly woke the driver up. I instructed the driver to turn the engine off and I approached the car. "ID cards please gentlemen."

As I was checking them all a purple faced Captain Bankmanager ran up and started to hop anxiously from foot to foot. I ignored him and after carefully checking all the ID's I gave a smart salute to the Brigadier and said, "Pass sir."

The captain then decided to berate me in front of everyone until the Brigadier cut him off in full flow. "Everything he did is what I would have expected, and he is a credit to your TA company."

Captain Bankmanager calmed down, thanked the Brigadier and started to walk off towards the mess. As the Brigadier walked past, I smiled and whispered, "I'm a regular Sir."

"Well done lad," he replied with the hint of a grin on his face. I never did find out what, if anything the Brigadier said to Captain BM, but he was very pleasant to me from then on.

Steve Morse, Sapper (Retired)

"The Navy is very old and very wise."
Rudyard Kipling

The grateful nation

In preparation for writing volume three I have bought and read dozens of books looking for interesting military stuff. (Honestly, the things I do for you.) And I found an interesting story in the account of the Falklands War written by Admiral Sandy Woodward. In my time in the army, it was easy to think we, the NCOs and ORs were always dumped on, and the officers were always cosseted and spoilt. Not so, as the following tale demonstrates.

As you probably know, Sandy Woodward was the Admiral in overall command of the British Forces during the Falklands War. Often called the cleverest man in the navy, the former submariner wrote a book about his experiences called 'One Hundred Days', a readable and gripping account of what he thought and felt during the conflict.

It must be remembered what this man did. The British put the Task Force together over a weekend and there were the typical cock ups and forgotten stuff that you would expect. He was completely missing certain types of ship that he needed (like minesweepers), he was being constantly hassled by the politicians, had to carry the knowledge that he was going to send men to their deaths and knew that if the mission was a failure, even if it was not his fault, he would be crucified by the press and the British public would never forgive him.

On top of this many countries were predicting that the British didn't have the wherewithal to remove the Argentinians and several ships including the Atlantic Conveyor were sunk en route taking lots of vital kit down with it. This made these countries (and lots of other countries now joined in) even more confident that Britain couldn't retake the Falklands.

But here's the thing. As we know he, and of course everyone else involved, did it. And in his own words, 'It was a damn close run thing.' The British had some luck, fair enough, but so did the Argies. As history has shown several times, there is no doubting the excellence of the British officers and men, and this was proven once again during that campaign.

So the hero returns, having achieved the almost impossible, and the Task Force is met by roaring crowds and the worlds press. Politicians are queueing up to have their photo taken with him the Queen later appointed him Knight Commander of the Order of the Bath (KCB) in recognition of service within the operations in the South Atlantic. Everyone loved him, everyone was grateful, and everyone wanted to be his mate and buy him a drink.

On his return to his office in Portsmouth there was a letter on his desk waiting for him. It was from the Director of Naval Pay and Pensions and had been posted five days before he had returned from the South Atlantic. Essentially it said that they had done a review of his expenditure on entertainment as part of his job for the last three months. (Taking no account of the fact that he had spent the last three months in the South Atlantic or that he had returned a hero.) The letter said as he had only spent a total of £5.85 during this time they were reducing his allowance by £1.78 a day.

The letter continued, 'Furthermore we have backdated this revision to that of your promotion in July 1981 last year. As a consequence you have been overpaid £649.70. We should be glad to receive payment of this, in full, at your earliest convenience.'

Welcome home sir. It's nice to know it wasn't just us.

Researched and written by Jonno DP.

Romance gone wrong

Me and my two buddies Barney and Tommo always used to head out and get ruined before an exercise. We were heading out early the next morning, so that evening we went down to the local Stadt, started in Cafe Fox and after a few in there went off to the Copper Kettle. After a few swift ones in there I got chatting to a local woman called Monica and we all enjoyed a few blow jobs. (A nickname for a drink in shot glasses with cream on top.) Monica was flirting like mad with me, kissing me and touching me up, then she announced she wanted us to take her back to camp. This is an idea that I was very keen on, but it was easier said than done as it would mean smuggling her through the gate, but worth a try. So the four of us got in a taxi and headed back to Lumsden Barracks, Barney in the front and me, Tommo and Monica in the back. We were trundling along, she's rubbing me up, and I am merrily groping her when she suddenly declared she wanted to have all of us at the same time. Barney was jealous of me getting all the action that night and so was particularly up for the idea of all three of us rattling her.

By now me and Monica are getting pretty full on so Tommo, being bored, decides to go through her bag for something to do. In the bag he found a camera and started taking pictures of the car behind us continuing with this activity after we had pulled up at the front gate. It's only when he is doing an arty low angle shot of the drivers window that the blue lights come on and we realise that it's some monkeys.

The RMPs didn't have to be detectives to realise that something was up and they called us over. I was still paying for the taxi so Barney started speaking to the male monkey and Monica was speaking to the female one. The RMPs quickly realised what the nights activities were going to be and decide to run Monica back into town. (Fucking killjoys. I swear monkeys lie awake at night haunted by the fear that someone, somewhere is having a good time). At this point, for reasons known only to himself and his psychiatrist, Tommo pissed all over the female RMPs shoes. Unsurprisingly, this changed the tone of the conversation, and we are now looking at getting well and truly nicked. Tommo saved the day though, he told the monkey he would clean it up then dropped to his knees and started licking his own piss of her shoes. Even I was gobsmacked by that one, and both the RMPs started laughing. In the end they decided to let us off with a warning, shame about Monica though.

James Terry

No Win Situation

When I was at school I was always a bit of a loner and consequently was happy with my own company.
Things were much the same when I joined the army, on the insistence of my father who had been a RSM during his time in the service. Once I had completed basic and trade training I was posted to Germany and upon my arrival I, like all new arrivals, had to have an interview with the commanding officer within the first few days so that he would have an idea of what job each new recruit was best suited for. He suggested that I might like to give the provost staff a go and I found that I enjoyed the work and took to it like the proverbial duck to water.
Each shift was composed of six soldiers like me with a corporal in charge, all the shifts being overseen by the provost sergeant and the RSM. I found I got on well with the rest of my shift as we were all of a similar type. The shift corporal noticed that I seemed happy with the job and after three months it was agreed that I would remain as permanent provost staff, much to my delight.
I was put forward for my first course, the Junior Military Qualifications course after a further month and as it was held in our own barracks it was easy to complete on my two day rest periods. I passed the course which qualified me for promotion, but I knew that it wasn't automatic and would probably take a while to achieve. In that I was quite wrong as thirteen months after joining the regiment I was promoted and given my own shift to oversee.
Around this time in the early nineteen seventies there was quite a lot of terrorist activity against British bases in Germany, mainly carried out by the IRA, not just against the army but also the RAF. In view of this the security was tightened up at all bases in Germany with added restrictions being placed on those people seeking admission to the barracks, whether

soldiers, German civilians or families. We were told that the gate security men had to check all ID cards even if it was someone we knew, regardless of rank with no exceptions. This point was emphasized. NO exceptions! This inevitably led to delays in the morning peak when soldiers and civilian workers were coming to work and queues quickly built up outside the gate as we checked everyone.

The first few days were difficult as the delays led to many soldiers being late on parade, which meant they got charged, but the situation was understood, and no fines or other punishments were actually handed out. Much to everyones relief they were just told to allow more time to get in to work in the mornings.

One evening I was sitting behind the guardroom desk at around seven forty five. I was aware that there was a major function taking place that evening at the officers mess with officers from other barracks, including the garrison headquarters attending. Just before eight 8 o'clock the gate man buzzed through to the guardroom on the internal phone and informed me that he had a staff car displaying one star outside the gate and that the officer in the rear seat, a Brigadier, was refusing to show his ID card. I went out to the gate and asked the driver for his ID and this was promptly displayed in the window for me to inspect. I saw through the windows that it was indeed a brigadier in the rear seat who was a regular visitor to the barracks. He often took lunch with the colonel and the three squadron majors and also sat as the principal officer at Court Martials at the district court martial centre, which was also within our barracks. Despite recognising him and knowing who he was I remembered the instruction that all IDs had to be shown with no exceptions. I went to the rear door, tapped on the window and requested his ID card. The Brigadier gave me a mouthful of abuse and said that he wasn't going to produce it as he was already late for the function. I hadn't saluted as I had decided to play everything by the book, reasoning that without the ID card he could have been anyone dressed in a brigadiers uniform. This seemed to annoy him even more. After three more polite requests for his ID card, all of which were refused, the brigadier got out of the staff car and angrily demanded to be let into the barracks. He was really losing it and I had visions of the situation actually resulting in violence on his part as he was really worked up by this point.

I now had a serious dilemma on my hands. Should I allow him to proceed into the barracks without a check? Or should I refuse entry and send him away? Or should I do what I would have done to any normal soldier who behaved like this? This option was immediate arrest and confinement in the guardroom.

I knew in my heart that I should go for the latter option and that whichever way I went it probably wasn`t going to end well for me. After some minutes of the brigadier blustering away right in my face, (I could actually feel his spit landing on my face as he ranted and swore at me) I decided I had had enough. I ordered the gate sentry to place him under arrest and to take him into the guardroom. The sentry looked at me as if I`d suddenly grown two heads and managed to stammer, "But corporal, he`s the brigadier."

"I`m well aware of that," I replied. "Now take him inside".

The sentry gulped and led the furious officer by the arm away from the car, through the personnel gate and along the short path to the guardroom door. I turned back to the staff car driver and told the driver that he wouldn`t be required and sent him away. When I got to the guardroom the brigadier was still shouting and demanding that he be allowed to proceed to the mess for the function. One of my team was an older Lance Corporal and had realised he was bulletproof because I had given the order, so he joined in with obvious glee. He was having no nonsense from the brigadier and curtly told him to empty his pockets onto the desk. A quick look by us confirmed that his ID card was not among his possessions.

That meant two charges, one for failing to carry a valid ID card and one for failure to produce the said card. After listing all his property we placed it in an envelope which was sealed and locked it in the safe at the back of the guardroom front office. I looked up at the board.

"Put him in cell eight." I said.

The brigadier was frogmarched along to the vacant cell by the happy lance corporal and two other shift members, pushed in and the door was slammed shut and locked. His shouts and rants could be heard all through the guardroom and the other resident prisoners were peeping round their cell doors to see what was afoot as it wasn't yet time for the doors to be locked for the night. I phoned the duty officer, a young second lieutenant and told him what I had done. The Officers Mess was about a quarter of a mile away from the guardroom and he arrived about ten seconds later panting hard with panic written all over his face.

After checking the property register and seeing that the ID card was not present he reluctantly agreed the charges stood. He walked up to the cell door and politely called through it. "Not a lot I can do sir. The charges stand as written so I will see you in the morning."

With that he went back to the party in the mess.

The following morning at six am we unlocked the cells so the prisoners could get washed and shaved before breakfast. The brigadier started ranting again but was just handed a razor, some soap and a towel, and told to join the other prisoners in the communal washroom and get shaved and dressed. He complained bitterly about all this but it fell on deaf ears.

We were due to hand over to another shift at nine so at eight thirty I went and unlocked his cell one more time and told him he was being released. He was still complaining that his breakfast had been half cold and barely eatable but guess what, no one cared. I returned his property and uniform jacket and said that he was free to go. The brigadier demanded to know where his car was and when I told him it had been sent away the previous evening, the ranting started all over again. He demanded that we let him use the duty Land-Rover to take him back to garrison headquarters and when this was refused his abuse went up another notch.

I assured him that transport wouldn't be a problem for him as there was a public bus stop across the road from the gate and that the buses ran every ten minutes, then I pushed him out the door and through the gate back onto the street.

I was very apprehensive about what would happen next and was pretty resigned to the fact that I could probably say goodbye to my stripes and would probably be thrown off the provost team as well. Talk about a no-win situation.

I was waiting for all hell to descend upon me, but days passed, I did more shifts and then it was a week in the past.

Just into my third shift since the incident the phone rang and I found myself talking to a full colonel at garrison headquarters who, it transpired, was a Major Generals adjutant. I was told to report to the headquarters at eleven that morning. I asked what dress I should wear, expecting to be told to wear full No 2s and be carrying enough washkit to keep me for several months in jail. But the colonel said normal working dress. Strange...

I took the duty Land Rover, headed across town to headquarters and on arrival was shown up into the Major Generals office. My heart sank when I saw the brigadier was also present. Ohhhh... here we go... The Major General told me to sit down, which I though was pretty unusual to say the least, and he began to speak.

"The brigadier would like to speak to you about an incident that took place at your barracks a week ago. Over to you Brigadier." The brigadier turned to face me, "Corporal, I was bloody annoyed with you the other night, in fact that is an understatement. Livid is probably a better word and I would have cheerfully shot you if I`d had a weapon handy! It caused me to miss an important function at the officers mess but now that I've calmed down I acknowledge I was in the wrong. I got dressed in a hurry and I forgot to transfer my ID card to my mess dress jacket. When I realised what I had done I thought I'd pull rank and try to bluster my way into the barracks. At the time, when you put me in a cell, I was going to make sure you lost your stripes, but all things considered, you acted entirely the right way. After all it was my directive you were following to the letter so any other course of action you might have chosen would probably would have resulted in demotion."

The Major general spoke up again, "Well corporal I have to say I admire your stance when faced with a difficult situation. I know you haven't been in Germany for that long, just over a year I believe, so it took some courage and conviction to carry out what you did. You'll be pleased to know that you're not losing your rank. Shake hands the two of you and then get back to your duties. We'll consider the matter closed."

"Thank you sir, I appreciate that. You too Brigadier, your apology is welcome and accepted."

All three of us stood up and I shook the brigadier by the hand, before saluting and turning to leave the office. The brigadiers parting words made me smile as I headed out of the office.

"I'll have to make sure I carry my ID card in future and god help me if I get on your wrong side again!"

That was really making the best of an impossible situation, my best choice as it turned out.

Cpl Chris Campbell 10 Regt RCT
More from Chris on the Facebook page "Chris Campbell - Author"

"Real friends don't get offended when you insult them, they just smile and call you something even more offensive."
Anon

Bird brain

Whilst I was in basic training in the ACC depot Aldershot, we were sent to the Tower Block Kitchen K1 to continue our trade training and the training Sergeant tasked a young female cook with roasting several trays of chickens. After about 15 minutes there's smoke, lots of smoke, and a really nasty plasticky pong coming from these ovens. We went across and opened the ovens releasing a huge choking cloud of smoke. People opened doors and windows or reached for fire extinguishers and the ovens were hurriedly turned off whilst we stood back and practised our swearing
After the smoke had dispersed somewhat we approached the ovens and found the cause of the problem, she had not unwrapped to birds from their packaging. Naturally enough, we asked why. Her reply was priceless, but strangely difficult to fault.
"It says oven ready on the packs and you told me to put them in the oven."
9/10, she did as she was told, however pulling the melted plastic off them before dinner seemed to take forever...

A-J ACC Attached to 21 Eng Reg. BFPO 48.

The Hohne Chronicles part 5. Social life.

There were lots of characters in 4 RHA. I remember one old Irish fella, who had been with the regiment for years was sitting in the Round House with me having morning tea when this loud mouthed yank starts spouting off. He was bragging about this tank they had that could travel 80 to 90 miles per hour overland. A load of bullshit, but he really was going on and on about it. Paddy, rolling a fag, starts to talk about the gunners in his regiment who were so fast at firing the guns that they could have four shells in the air before the first one landed. These yanks were just sitting there with their mouths open. He goes on to say that the first three were made of rubber and the last one was high explosive. Silent, they are even more amazed, he has them in his grasp. He continued, "The first three hit the tank in the door, knock, knock, knock, you see. And when the gunner opens the hatch to see who it is, in goes the high explosive shell and destroys the tank."
It took a while before they realised he had been taking the piss and when they did, he offered to take away the rubber shells from his story if they would take 40 miles per hour off of theirs.
The Social Side of Life at Hohne. There wasn't one.
So off duty soldiers would leave camp, drink vast amounts of alcohol, then return. I had a mate who was the Recovery Mechanic for 4 RHA and was forever being called out on a Saturday night for the recovery of an old cannon belonging to Mercer Troop that had been chucked in the swimming pool by drunken soldiers. This happened a lot around about the time of the Schutzenfest. The cannon was on proud display right next to a swimming pool, so it was a prank waiting to happen. I know officers are meant to be clever, but I think soldiers are way smarter, there probably wasn't a soldier in the entire regiment who would have suggested putting it there. The drunks would unchain the cannon from its mounting, drag it

over to the swimming pool, shove it in and run off giggling. The Colonel was furious every time it happened. This cannon was his pride and joy and had been with the Regiment ever since it had been captured from Napoleon's boys at the Battle of Waterloo. No respect at all. Many a time 4th RHA would be confined to barracks for their antics.

The main gate when you turned into camp was flanked by the 26th Armoured Engineers and 14/20th King's Hussars, and then the road led straight down to the Roundhouse and the cinema. There was another gate further along the fence towards Belsen, which was 4th RHAs gate, and it was outside this gate that the infamous Snake Pit boozer was situated. To my recollection there was also a tattoo parlour around the back of it and it was a dangerous place for drunken soldiers who had just spent all day drinking in Bergen. Many a squaddie woke up with sore arms wondering what had happened!

There was another pub over on the tank ranges called Range 4 and it was quite a walk to get there. I can remember walking down and back many a night watching the Honest John rockets tracing their way through the night sky to the target, and also being chased by wild pigs on the way back – yes, pigs – not pink elephants! I spent quite a lot of time down at Range 4 for good reason. I was romancing this fraulein by the name of Elke Phillips who lived in the nearby village. I actually proposed to her at one stage, but fortunately she had enough sense to turn me down. Her actual answer to my proposal was a letter saying, "De ehe ist kinderspiele." It means "Your idea of marriage is a childs game." Short and to the point, it's funny how you remember these things. Ah, well!

Towards the end of my time in Hohne when National Service was just about finished, 4th RHA changed its role and became the 7th Para RHA and was posted to Hong Kong, so a lot of my mates left. They were replaced with the 25th Medium Regiment Royal Artillery who were returning after a stint in Cyprus. My god they were a wild bunch once they were let loose in the town! They wrecked the Berger-Hof pub one night, but it was the landlord's own fault. He switched off the jukebox after these guys had filled it up with money, so they tore it off the wall and he locked the glass doors with us all inside, silly man. The Monkeys had quite a time trying to round up all the culprits who by this time were all over Bergen.

There was another pub up the road to the right, just past the grounds where the Schutzenfest was held every year. It was always good for a cheap feed anytime, day or night, although I cannot remember its name, and there was a hardware store around the corner from the Berger Hof. I remember it, because the owner's daughter, a redhead called Inga, used to work at the camp Post Office next door to our signal centre and she had translated my letter of rejection from Elke Phillips. Of course, she took great delight in telling all my buddies and the guys in the post office. I felt a right turkey.

All was not lost for female company though! Me and a mate were on our way back to camp one Saturday night in his car and I spotted a young lady walking in the same direction. She had her head bowed and looked like she was upset so I get him to stop the car. Sir Galahad jumps out and asks the fair maiden what her plight is. Her name was Annalaura and she had nowhere to sleep and was looking for somewhere to doss down. Being gallant I stuffed her into the back of the Volkswagen and we went on our merry way back to camp. It was after midnight and we managed to sneak her through the main gate hidden under a pile of jackets. We drove down through the camp to the Roundhouse and knocked on the door of the YMCA billets. The matron opened the door in a bit of a daze and asked what was up. I gave her a sob story about how I had found this poor unfortunate being, wandering cold and miserable with nowhere to sleep. It worked. She took her in for the night and off we went feeling really proud of ourselves. What heroes!

I went down to the Roundhouse the next morning about lunch time for a coffee and there is this young lady serving behind the counter. The boss lady had given her a job and a place to sleep till she could get settled. Wow, I was the hero of the day and Annalaura couldn't do enough for me. After a few days she got settled in the town with a nice little flat and a job at the Berger Hof bar as a waitress and barmaid. As well as helping her I had certainly done myself a favour too. I got the odd free beer and meal, and also started to go out with her! Life was sweet till I stuffed it up, I remember it well.

Things were fine between us until the Schutzenfest hit town. It was a week long annual festival with open air dances, a fairground and shooting galleries, a lavish affair. It was my birthday, so I had put my best rags on and treated myself to a taxi to the Berger Hof in Bergen. I got out looking elegant and debonair and slammed the taxi door on my thumb. The air turned blue and so did my thumb after a bit. The screaming pain did wear off after a while and settled down to a painful throb and after a couple of hours drinking I was oblivious. Off we go to the Schutzenfest and Jock Kelly and I decided to show the Germans our skill at jiving. The Germans were very traditional in their ways, all dressed in their lederhosen and the music was 'Um pa, Um pa' and very boring. They were not pleased with two guys dancing together, and it was not long before the Polizei turned up. We were taken to one side and told that it was a no-no. Ok, back to the bar.

Not long after that Annalaura arrived after finishing her shift at work, but by then I was away with the fairies. I asked her for a dance, but she declined saying I was not really in a fit state for dancing. Jock got her up to dance instead, he didn't drink very much at all, and when they came back I was jealous and started calling her names. That was the end of another wonderful friendship and the end of the free drinks. German lager has a lot to answer for.

I had a final weird experience at Hohne on my last night before I was to return to Verden. Whilst being in Hohne I had made friends with a corporal from the Royal Engineers and his wife Stella, and they organised a party for me and my mates down at their place in the married quarters starting at 9 o'clock. I went NAAFI for a few gins beforehand, but I made sure the lads did not spike my drinks because it was going to be a long evening, and I had to catch a truck to Verden at 1.30am. I left the NAAFI at about 8.30, jumped on my mate's pushbike and started the ten minute ride to the house where the party was going to be. I was the guest of honour and should be there to greet everyone as they arrived. I parked the bike and knocked on the door. A surprised Stella greats me with, "Where the hell have you been?" She then explains that everyone has gone home and it just after midnight. To this day I do not know what happened between leaving the NAAFI on the bike and arriving three to four hours later. I had no signs of scuff marks from falling off the bike or grass marks from sleeping in the paddocks.

After a quick farewell and lots of apologies I raced back to my barracks to pick up my gear and jump on the overnight mail truck back to my regiment in Verden.

L/Cpl J.B. Travers. 207 Signals Squadron. 7th Armoured Brigade 1960/61.

My toy! MINE!

My first posting was 71 Aircraft Workshop REME in Detmold in 1978 and after I had been there a while the hangar went through a refurbishment. It still had the original brick floor and in the girders above you could still see shell and shrapnel holes in the metalwork from the war. During the refurbishment a new 10-ton Demag crane was fitted that would cover the whole of the workshop floor. We were all desperate to have a go on it but a notice soon appeared on the crane controls saying, "Only senior NCOs and above are allowed to use this crane".

We soon found out that every time the crane moved (it was quite noisy) one of the AQMS from the avionics bay would gallop out of the office to see who was using their precious, keen on checking the user was of the required rank or to tear a strip off some poor sod.

So it became a game to walk past the control and move the crane a few metres and then leg it and hide. Then, said AQMS would rush out to see his precious crane controls swinging gently with no-one in sight. We would do this at random times during the day over a week or so and it got to him so much that after one sneaky moving of his crane he shouted at an empty hangar, "Will you bastards stop doing that!!"

Ah good. Its working!

Shortly after this the notice disappeared, training was organised, and the riff raff were allowed to use the crane.

Ian Payne (REME Aviation)

'It is foolish to mourn the men who died. Rather, we should thank God that such men lived.'
George Patton Jr

Speak up sir!

I have just been reading your second volume 'We were cold warriors 2', so being an ex gunner and a stalwart driver I will tell you of my own adventure driving an Arty Limber on a night occupation in Germany in the late 1970s.

We pulled up to the edge of a wood somewhere on Soltau ranges, pitch black, couldn't see a bloody thing. Then I see a light moving up and down. (Editors note, manoeuvring vehicles in pitch darkness is as dangerous as it sounds, so masked torches, and sometimes lit cigarettes, were used to signal a driver in darkness without advertising our presence to any enemy. Different movements meant different manoeuvres, for example a circular motion means reverse and the light going out means stop.) The light I was seeing was an up and down motion which means advance, so moving very slowly forward I followed it until it went out. I sat and waited for any further instructions and became aware of a knocking on my splash board on the front of the truck. 'Maybe he's wants me to cam-up?' I thought. Being unsure I opened the hatch and looked down to the front of my stollie. The tapping was clearer now and I could see that the guy who had guided me in was trapped between a tree and the front of my stollie!

I pulled back slowly and a hoarse Irish voice floated up and said, "Cam-up." Then he disappeared into the night. The next morning I was at the Q wagon and the BSM jumped on to a hay box, pointed at me and said in a voice like a hellfire preacher, "Never, ever guide this fucking nutcase in on a night 'cause he will try and kill you!"

A bit harsh I thought, but overnight I became a legend within the Battery! (In the following years I nearly claimed another BSM and a TSM)

Scoobie 49 Battery, 40 Field Regt

Rolling, rolling, rolling...

You might thing driving a TTF (fuel tanker) was a bit of a boring job, but not so. The first time I heard of an interesting incident with them was when a guy I knew parked his TTF during Exercise Lionheart in 1984 and went to his pit for the night. He came back in the morning and there it was – gone! He thought one of his mates was taking the piss and had moved it, but it slowly dawned on him that this was not the case. It was finally found in the river Weser about a mile downstream sitting neatly on the riverbed and could only be detected by disturbed water above it. If you know anything about Germans you will appreciate just how much they were freaking out over the prospect of thousands of gallons of diesel leaking into one of their major rivers, but credit to 28 Amphibious Engineer Squadron, they pulled it out without spilling any.
(If you want to see photos check out https://british-army-in-hameln.com/1984-exercise-lionheart-real-recovery-operation/ - Jonno DP)
My interesting day was April the 1st 1985, that's right April fool's day, and I was in 33 Squadron Royal Corps of Transport Stationed in Bunde and attached to the 2nd Royal Tank Regiment in Fallingbostel whilst their fuel point was being refurbished. Basically my job was to refuel all their tanks (thirsty beasts chieftains) as long as their POL point was out of service. When I ran dry I went off refill the 12,000-litre tanker, and as it was April Fools Day several people called out after me to point this out and to tell me to be careful I didn't have an accident.
The TTF was a double H plate meaning it was quite new and was a pretty good drive, but after I filled her up and was on my way back I did have an accident and it was a bit of a corker! I had just come up to the top of a hill in fifth gear when the truck swerved to the left then swerved to the right and wasn't

answering the steering wheel at all. After the last swerve it rolled over four times and ended up on up its side. In Germany roads often have ditches along the sides of them and after it tipped over for the last time it slid sideways straddling the ditch with the back end on one side and the front end on the other. Fortunately it was diesel I was carrying, which is far less flammable than petrol, but 12,000 litres is a lot and if that starts leaking out everywhere it's going to make a hell of a mess. Amazingly the only fuel that was spilt, was in the vehicles own fuel tank which was ripped off when the vehicle rolled. I didn't know most of this at the time because I was chucked headfirst through the driver's window on the fourth roll knocking me out and putting me in hospital for 6 days. Had it rolled a fifth time I would have been underneath it, so overall I was lucky I suppose.

There was one eyewitness to the accident, a German lady who was driving her car towards me, and her witness statement said that when the steering went and the TTF was all over the place I was sat there with folded arms and a resigned expression on my face looking like I was thinking, 'Oh here we go'. I did have a real stroke of luck though, a German ambulance was two or three vehicles behind me so it didn't take long before I was on my way to hospital.

As I said I don't remember much, I remember driving on the road and the next thing I know I was waking up in the German krankenhaus. I was really lucky that the ambulance was so close behind me, but I had some bad luck that day too. I had glass embedded in my head, but on the other hand I hadn't been wearing a seatbelt which had prevented me from being impaled by one of the window bars. Despite being bashed up and unconscious the German ambulance crew and the medics in the hospital gave me no medical treatment whatsoever, not even a drip. They just put me in bed and left me there. When a medical team in a military ambulance turned up from BMH

Hanover they went absolutely mental at them for the lack of care.

My next set of visitors had a less caring attitude however, it was a couple of Military Police who promptly charged me with dangerous driving and failing to wear a seatbelt. To be fair to them, after they visited the crash site and had a look they did come back and say the charges would be dropped.

I was later told (as I said I don't remember the actual accident at all) that I was in fifth gear, doing no more than 30 MPH and that despite it being a nearly new truck with less than 8000 miles on the clock the steering box had collapsed. It turned out that I was luckier than I thought at the time. Two other Foden TTFs also had steering boxes collapse. Mine was the first, the second one had one fatality and the third one had two including the driver.

Funnily enough, I now work for Foden and one of my workmates is ex 2 RTR and remembers the accident. Small world.

Derek Golding, 33 Squadron RCT, Bunde.

Oops! Sorry sir.

We did the very last ever firing camp with the 40/70 bofors gun, an old anti-aircraft gun that had replaced the World War 2 anti-aircraft artillery in the late forties. By the 1970s it was showing its age and we were going to be reequipped with the rapier AA missile system, but as I said, we had one more firing camp to go. The general idea at a firing camp was that a Canberra aircraft would tow a target in front of us on a long rope (a very long rope) and we would shoot at it.

We had 6 guns in our battery, and there were two more with us from the Gibraltar Regiment. After some live firing the Canberra pilot contacted us to tell us to check firing as he had to move around and sort out his towed target. So we were marched away from the guns to sit down and have a brew and a smoke.

But unbeknownst to us one of the Gibraltar guns had a hang fire, and on this type of gun the SOP was to wait 20 minutes before attempting to unload it. If you made a list of things that artillerymen don't like, a hang fire is probably top of the list. A hang fire is when you have attempted to fire an artillery gun (or any large gun) and the propellant hasn't gone bang and shoved the shell down the barrel. It may be because there is a problem with the firing mechanism etc, or it may be that everything mechanical worked fine and it will go bang without warning in ten minutes, or twenty. Or an hour. The problem is you need to get the gun firing again, so you don't have the option of leaving it a day or two, you have to manually unload it, and of course if this coincides with the propellant going off it's going to blow you to smithereens.

We didn't know this; we were sitting back from the guns in our gun subs watching the Canberra lining up to tow the target in front of the guns. Range control called 'RANGE OPEN, RANGE

OPEN!" and we were waiting for our gun number ones to order us to take post.

It was then that the gun to our extreme right, the Gibraltar gun with the hang fire, went BOOOOOOOOMMMMMM............

It was close, very close, and we saw the Canberra pilot instinctively yank the plane into a bank. We think he must have felt the shell pass close because absolutely outraged he came up on the radio with, "OY YOU BASTARDS I AM PULLING THIS FUCKING THING, NOT PUSHING IT!!" So pissed of was he that he and his plane fucked off for the day and didn't come back. That was it, range closed! Bloody spoilsport.

Blackie 16 Air Defence Regiment Royal Artillery

Just plain sailing

There was an RCT dinghy sailing regatta at the Dummer See in Germany in the summer of, I think, 1991. Part of the trick of dinghy sailing is to bump into somebody making it look like their fault and someone who I shall call Captain S did this to me during the race, so a protest was raised about whose fault it was.

I asked the captain what time the hearing was, but he just gave me a superior look and said it might be at two in the morning. I couldn't hang around indefinitely, so I got on my motorbike and did the 45-minute ride back to camp intending to go back later for the hearing. When I got back to camp I was amazed to discover that Captain S had phoned up the guard commander and told him to have me jailed, although the actual charges were left somewhat vague. Fortunately for me the duty officer was the unit quartermaster (Captain W) who was a great bloke and someone I often went sailing with. Also, I was a Lance Jack, and you can't just jail a Lance Jack with no charge.

He had me released, but there must have been some kind of hearing presided over by the Brigadier because I ended up being banned from sailing for the RCT for one year. Charming. I never even had a chance to say my piece, he just swallowed the shit that Captain S gave him. I was also told that if I wanted to sail again for the RCT *after* the one year ban was up I would need to reapply for permission to be allowed to do it.

I never did bother reapplying for permission to sail for the RCT because not long after this the unit was disbanded, and I was posted to a REME workshops as the OC workshops driver which was a fantastic job. I only drove him a couple of times in the two years I was there and ended up spending most of my time with the reccy mechs.

Some high ranking REME officer (I think it was a general, but my memory may be faulty) organised a sailing regatta on the

Mohnesee called the brass hat Regatta. (One of the dams smashed by the dambusters is there.) Now, the OC of this unit knew that I used to sail so he put me forward for it. Off I went to the regatta, had a look at the list of competitors and saw the name of the Brigadier who had banned me for sailing. Hmmmm....

So the race started, and off we went. Now, remember that the idea is that you get very close and even bump into one of your competitors, and also bear in mind that these two man sailing dinghies are absolutely tiny. We started to gain on one boat in front of us although the speed differential was small. Eventually we overtook him, and we did it at a crawl. I took my eyes off the sail and glanced across to the person in the other boat. Surprise! It was crewed by the Brigadier who banned me from sailing for the RCT! I gave him a little wave, but he didn't wave back.

I bumped into him later that day in the changing rooms but he didn't say a single word to me. I found out later that he didn't speak to me because he was absolutely furious that I would sail for the REME and not for the RCT. Sometimes the universe just rights itself!

Lance Corporal Simon Martell 54 Squadron RCT Lubecke

You can't park that there...

I was in an RA Regiment based in Munsterlarger in the early 1970s and one day we had been live firing our Abbot Self Propelled Artillery guns on Hohne ranges. After endex was given we packed up and started to move back to camp via the Hohne ring road. I was the gun commander (called the number 1 in the Artillery) and was standing up in the No1 hatch, and my coverer was standing in the No2 hatch, my brother was on my crew and was sitting in the layers seat below me.

Two other crew were sitting inside the gun and doing what we always did whilst driving along after live firing, they were stripping the breech block ready for cleaning to save time when we got back into camp. If you don't know, the breech block is the bit that closes over the end of the barrel after you have loaded the gun. It takes the pressure of the gun firing so it's a hefty chunk of metal that requires careful moving if you don't like squashed fingers.

As we were traveling along the ring road at about 30mph the gun kept veering over to the left, so I got on the intercom to the driver. "What are you doing man? Why do you keep going left?"

"It's not me, the gun is doing it by itself!" he called back.

Just then the gun jerked sharp left and hit a tree that had been minding its own business on the edge of the road. The Abbot hit it square on in the middle of the hull and started to go vertical, the tracks still trying to push it forward.

The gun kept going up and started tilting over to the left. Just in time I shouted at my coverer, "GET DOWN!!" and we dived inside the turret. The gun rolled over completely upside down and when everything stopped flying around I found myself sitting upside down in my seat with my head touching grass, my brother on top of me and one of the internal batteries emptying itself over us.

The tracks were still flying around at speed, so I shouted for someone to switch the engine off. (There is an engine switch in the back of the gun.) They were a bit disorientated as the gun was upside down and in pitch darkness so it took a while for them to find it, but they got it in the end and switched it off. Incredibly, no one was hurt. As we had gone over all the loose items inside the gun had gone flying around, and by a miracle no one had a part of their anatomy squashed flat by the breech block. We all
managed to get down out of our upside-down seats so we were standing on the inside of the turret. I could hear someone banging on the handle trying to open the back door but not realizing that they were locking the door more as the handle was now upside down.

In the end the number 1 from the gun behind us, who had seen what happened, came over and kicked the door handle the right way, letting us tumble out into sunlight and fresh air.

In an Abbott the turret batteries are under the layers seat, so as we rolled over the acid spilled all over me and my brother and our combats were already full of holes and falling to bits.

All of us in the back of the gun were ok, but I was really worried about my driver in the front. By another piece of amazing luck, when we hit the tree he was thrown out the drivers cab and the gun *just* missed him as it rolled over. His back was hurting him where he had pulled a muscle, but apart from that everyone was ok.

We got a lift back to camp and we all went straight in the NAAFI and had a double whiskey each. We just could not believe our luck that no one had suffered even a minor injury. A later investigation showed that the steering box on the left track had gone and the driver had no control of the track, so it was absolutely not his fault.

The worst thing about it was that when I got my gun back I had to spend about a week removing 300 odd screws on the flotation screen as this was the only thing that was damaged. Once that was done, I spent another week putting the new one back on.

Ernie Dobson 4th Regiment RA

'Freedom is never free.'
Anon

Safe as houses here

I was born in Brooklyn, New York in the 1970s and when I was young we moved to Long Island about twenty miles outside the city. One of the reasons we moved there was because my parents were pretty anti-nuclear weapons and they thought we would be safer from nuclear attack if we were further away. This was a thing that occupied a lot of American thoughts back then. My Elementary school, Junior High School, and High School all had nuclear fallout shelters in them built to a 1950s Cold War code. From ground level you had to go down, down, down many flights of stairs to get to the bottom. It's a rifle range now. (I know, how American!) Up until the early seventies we even had to wear dog tags with our name and social security number on it. These were made to be resistant to heat so after everyone had emptied their arsenals of nuclear missiles at each other someone could pick up a dog tag next to a scorch mark on a wall and say, "Well, that used to be Will Angeloro!" That was the theory anyway, but I couldn't see it myself.

I have lived and worked in Britain for decades now and I have discovered that my younger years were a lot different from the British experience. For example, every week we would have to take part in civil defence drills at school where we would get under our desks to protect us as if we were under nuclear attack. I wasn't eager to do this for several reasons. Firstly getting under a desk didn't seem like a skill that I would need to practice, secondly compared to sitting on my chair, I wasn't convinced that an old wooden desk would give me much extra protection from a nuclear fireball and thirdly I'm a big guy now, and I was a big boy then, so trying to cram myself under the desk was an uncomfortable thing to do.

We were often shown cartoons of Burt the Turtle doing 'duck and cover' which even to my childish eyes seemed unlikely to save me if a nuclear weapon landed anywhere near. (Editors note: - Google Burt the Turtle, it's hilarious.) Even in the seventies and eighties when I was growing up Burt the Turtle and Duck and Cover seemed very antiquated because it was talking about huge fleets of bombers flying across and dropping nuclear bombs on everybody. Of course by the time I was in school it was ICBMs that would have rained down on us. It seems comical now, but it used to literally give me nightmares about nuclear attack and any attempt to take cover seemed futile.

As I said, at the time we got some comfort thinking we would be safer outside the city, it would still be terrible, but we thought maybe we would survive a nuclear attack. But of course now we know we wouldn't have stood a chance, the whole place would have been devastated as back then the centre of long Island was the heart of the massive American aerospace industry. It was only in the nineties that we realised that we had been surrounded by a series of massive bullseyes and that in the event of nuclear attack our neighbourhood would have been a huge smoking crater, or more likely, a series of overlapping craters.

Anyway, fast forward to the late 1990s, well after the end of the Cold War. I was visiting my parents on Long Island and I heard about a strange story that put even this sad and silly tale in the shade. To understand what happened, you need to know a little about American social history. On the worst bits of land in the greater New York area they put airports, refuse dumps, cemeteries and housing for non-white people. Then the banks that loaned people money to buy houses drew red lines around these neighbourhoods and refused to give mortgages to anyone wanting to move out of a poor neighbourhood into a nice one effectively creating ghettoes and perpetuating the segregation of races. This stopped a long time ago and some of these so called 'redlined' neighbourhoods are really nice now. The ethnicity is now much more mixed and this limiting of mortgages doesn't happen anymore, but the upsetting memory of the redline still exists, particularly amongst the older population.

When I was visiting there was a church in a former redline area called Farmingdale that had an exclusively black congregation that applied for planning permission to put a two storey extension on top of their church. They didn't think this would be a problem as only a few hundred yards away a predominantly white church had been granted similar permission with no problems at all. To their surprise this request was turned down and naturally enough they asked why it was that a white church could get permission and a black church could not. The planning authorities agreed that it was strange but they informed the church goers that there was a decades old confidential clause on the deeds saying they could never build higher than one storey. As this had been on there a long time no one in the planning office had any idea why it would be there, but they would investigate and see if it could be lifted. The church was near to an airport, but three storeys in total was not much, and it was far enough from the airport for the height to not be an issue at all.

The reasons for this clause were probed and it was discovered that the US department of defence had put a block on any building higher than one story where the church was, and also on some surrounding buildings. This just mystified people all the more. Why the hell would the department of defence be interested how high these places could be? Further investigation revealed why, and it floored everybody. The reason was, and bear in mind nobody knew this at the time, that the American military had secretly built a Nike anti-ballistic nuclear missile base right in the middle of the redline zone. The base was an Air National Guard site that was tacked onto the side of Republic Airport, which was a small civilian airport. In America it's common for civilian airports have a detachment of the Air National Guard with it, which is how they managed to excavate the silos, pour concrete and bring the missiles in without anybody knowing. The height limits on the nearby buildings were there so the line of sight for launching these missiles would remain clear.

And these weren't just small missiles to shoot down incoming Russian nukes, these were themselves multistage nuclear missiles designed to give a colossal explosion very high in the atmosphere, thereby shattering multiple incoming Russian intercontinental ballistic missiles. Further investigation showed that this secret site contained 10 of these Nike missiles (later upgraded to the Hercules missiles) and each of these missiles carried a 10 kiloton nuclear warhead. (Editor's note: - To put this into perspective the bomb that was dropped on Hiroshima was sixteen kilotons.) Once this was known other questions were immediately asked. Why where they placed in Long Island? Why not somewhere else in New York? And why New York? The answers to these questions took away whatever breath the nearby residents had left. New York was studded with these bases, ringed by them in fact, and Long Island itself had more than one. And it wasn't just New York either. Other important population centres and military sites were protected by multiple missile bases too, a total of almost 300 sites in the continental United States altogether. And the entire time they were there, no one had any idea whatsoever. I think back to all the people who protested about nuclear power stations being built and they would have had no idea that thy were quite possibly living very close to a hundred kilotons worth of warheads. At the end of the Cold War the sites were quietly dismantled and the missiles taken away, but no one had thought to remove the limitation on extending the church. Had they done, it's likely, indeed probable, that people would never have found out that they had been living next door to nuclear weapons. None of this came out until 1997 and 1998 and then you could go and have a look at all the concrete emplacements for the missiles

I had personally lived about eight miles east of this missile site right smack in the centre of Long Island. Now we know more about the Cold War it seems very likely the Soviets would have known about this place meaning it would certainly have been an important target for them, so at least I have the satisfaction of being right about the pointlessness of cramming myself under the desk.

Will Angeloro (Mate of Jonno DP)

Drink! Drink! Drink!

I was a bit of a naughty boy when I was younger and wasn't allowed to join the army, so I joined the TA instead. I was always a bit of a wheeler dealer making money at car boot sales and things and I continued this after the TA sent me to Afghanistan in 2010. At that time you could buy Turkish rugs for about $50 that would sell in the UK for several hundred quid, but there was a problem. You can only send about two kilograms of weight back to the UK through the British Forces post office system so I would hitch a lift over to the Danish and send it through their post office system which had no weight limit. In the end I made about 5 grand out of that.

I got more ambitious after that and was going through the process to buy a local motorcycle for next to nothing and send it back to the UK bit by bit, but unfortunately someone cottoned on to what I was doing and put the kibosh on it.

I did still branch out though and started my own brewery in a sanger. I got a relative of mine in the UK to send me some Malibu mouthwash. This is great stuff, it smells and tastes just like Malibu rum, but is a different colour. So I would get one of my relatives to carefully open the Malibu mouthwash, empty the contents, rinse it out, refill it with real Malibu and put some food flavouring in it. Honestly you just couldn't tell the difference until you started drinking it. Many a happy night.

Then I decided to branch out into something bigger. I got one of my friends in the UK to send me some brewers yeast, crazy straws, and other bits of kit useful to brewers (I come from a family of brewers, so I knew what I was doing) I also had a chat with some Fijian lads who had some great big tubs of fruit juice. There was a sangar almost in the middle of camp that I quietly requisitioned and off I went. A bucket was sterilised, the process of brewing was started. I had to stir it every day for five days, strain it etc but after about two weeks, hey presto! I had a couple of gallons of what tasted like apple wine. I needed an excuse to keep going in and out of the sangar so I asked the guy in charge of duties if I could do some sangar bashing. He was a bit puzzled why, but a promise of some booze smoothed the path there. In the end I was using so much fruit juice to make booze for everyone the shop put a limit on how much one person could have each purchase. I kept this going for months!

Ian Coulthard 3LSR

A very bad day

On the 28th of February 1992 I was with 4th Troop, C Squadron, 4/7 Royal Dragoon Guards crewing chieftains in Hobart Barracks Detmold and we were in camp spraying the vehicles ready for amalgamating with the 5th Skins. Funny isn't it? Everybody knows they're all fucked but you just spray them better with some paint and off you go. Anyway, on this day someone else was spraying the vehicles better and I had to take an old samson vehicle in the hangars down to the LAD, but what they hadn't told us was that it was VOR. Worse, they haven't told us was that it was VOR for the brakes.

Now if you don't know, if you move a vehicle on camp you must have somebody either commanding it as you do when you drive it on the road, or somebody guiding it like those people who guide aircraft on a runway. If you had to take the vehicle a long distance you would literally walk in front of it and the vehicle would trundle along behind.

So with Trev Trevelyan driving and me walking in front of it we got it down to the LAD and I started backing it over a pit. I had to do a bit of a dogleg to get him in and I could see he was about to clip a tank so I pulled him forward to straighten him up and this is when I discovered why the samson was VOR. Trev couldn't stop the vehicle and it rolled straight into me crushing my pelvis up against the front bumper of a Bedford RL.

Now a samson weighs about nine tons and an RL weighs about four and a half. It had the handbrake on fully, but such was the force of the samson hitting the RL (with me as a cushion of course) it still moved it back about six feet. My pelvis was broken in four places and shoved it up six inches towards my rib cage. I started screaming my bollocks off, and remained conscious throughout the entire incident, but by the time they moved the samson back I was pretty much out of it. To be honest I was kind of lucky, had it been a 10 tonner, which has a higher bumper than an RL, it would have been my rib cage that was crushed and I would have been killed outright.

The army flew my mum and dad out to BMH Rinteln the day after the accident and one of the only upsides to the entire event was watching my dad lay into the colonel. Me and a load of other lads had been on orders not that long ago for getting up to various antics which I thought had been made too much of, so watching dad bollocking the colonel, who had no defence at all for what had happened, was quite amazing. At first he tried giving my dad a load of old shit about, "Unfortunate accident... totally unforeseen... nothing could have been done... chance in a million... these things happen..." etc, but my dad is from the north of England and has the accent and attitude to go with it.

He waited until the colonel had finished his spiel and came back loudly with, "Nah then. What you're fucking telling me is you got one of your NCOs to tell my son to bring a vehicle down to the LAD from a maintenance park when it was VOR. And you didn't tell him that it was VOR cos the fucking brakes didn't work."

"Mr Mitchell." said the colonel, "Did you happen to have been in the army?"

Dad said, "Yes I was."

The colonel said, "Oh fuck." (These were his exact words.)

The surgeon told my dad that had I arrived in hospital five minutes later he would have been coming for my funeral and not to visit me in hospital. After I woke up I remember being surrounded by people, maybe my parents, but I can't remember as I was off my tits on morphine. My pelvis was broken in four places, my spleen had burst, I had a blood clot in my bladder, and I lost seven pints of blood internally on the way to BMH Rinteln.

I was six months in intensive care, and it was 18 months before the army considered me fully fit again. In the end I never really did get fully fit, but the army refused to give me a medical discharge. I did get compensation for the accident after a long slog, and hopefully there will be no long term effects, but of course you never know when it's going to come back as you get older.

This accident finished my career in the army and I ended up suing them. You would think considering all the factors that this would be pretty straightforward, but it took eight years and the army fought it all the way.

There was a huge enquiry about the accident later on, but they couldn't call the colonel. He'd retired shortly after the accident.

Paul Mitchell, 4/7 Royal Dragoon Guards, Detmold.

You took your time...

I was a lance jack in 206 Squadron, 3 UK div HQ and it was decided that the unit would go adventure training in France somewhere. I think it was Val d'Isere, but I couldn't swear to it, you know how it is.
We had a great time on the adventure training and the last night was St. Patricks Day (this was 2005) and I went out and got totally shitfaced. We had all been told that the transport was leaving at ten the following morning and we had-had-had to be there as the transport needed to leave to make the ferry on time. Well, on St. Paddys night I had one too many sips of the old lemonade and the next thing I remember is on waking up in some kind of dormitory. It was the kind that international guest workers sleep in and I'm on the floor with some random bird when the supervisor came in and kicked us awake, literally kicked us until we were awake. The girl jumped up because the boss is there and she's trying to get herself all sorted out so she can get off and do whatever job she needs to do. So while she's getting yelled at by the boss in German for bringing a bloke back I got dressed and slipped out the door.
It was only when I got outside and sighed a sigh of relief that I realised I had no idea where I was and no idea what time it was. Literally no clue. I had become quite familiar with the village and the close countryside that we'd been staying in, but I'm looking around and absolutely nothing is ringing any bells. There were people walking around in full ski kit, you know, salopettes goggles and all that stuff, and I'm walking around in a t-shirt and jeans in about minus ten degrees. I remembered that I had had a coat when I'd left to go out drinking last night, fuck knows where that ended up.
I wandered around aimlessly for a bit looking for something familiar, but nothing. In the end I asked somebody if they knew the way to our accommodation, I remembered the name of

that at least. I was lucky that the person I asked not only knew the way but ended up giving me a lift there! It was a good fifteen minutes drive from where I was to get back to where we were staying so how I managed to get so far away last night, god knows. I was dropped off in the village and quickly found my way back to the building that we've been staying in. I walked into the foyer and thought, 'It's a bit quiet in here'.
I asked the receptionist if she had a key to my room, (that had gone missing as well), and she refused to give one to me. It was then that realisation dawned on me. Oh shiiiiiiiit!!!! They've gone haven't they? But all was not lost, the receptionist handed over a carrier bag that contained my passport, forty-seven euros in loose change and the leather jacket that I thought I'd lost last night. No wallet, no bank cards, just what I was standing in and what she had just given to me. And I was stuck in the south of France. There was, however, a note. It said something like,
'You've missed the transport. We waited an hour. The lads had a whip round and if you're not back by Monday you will be in my office.'
This was Saturday morning. well late-morning to be honest.
I felt absolutely minging like you do when you wake up from a night out and I decided to try to sneak back into my room to see if I can have a quick wash to make myself feel better. Hopefully I had a good time that night, but I can remember fuck-all about it.
It proved impossible to sneak into my room, so I decided to try and front it out with the receptionist. I told her I had left a valuable item in the room and would it be possible for me to just nip in and have a quick look for it. I piled on the old charm and in the end she caved and gave me a key. In I went. Of course I took full advantage of this, I stripped off had a quick shower and dried myself on my t-shirt so I didn't mess up their new towels.

I was absolutely starving so I went to the cafe in the village and ordered a ton of food and a few beers. This racked up a cost of about 70 euros and when they went to fetch the bill I legged it. I'm not sure if they chased me, I was still quite pissed to be honest.

I went to the bus station in the village and asked where the nearest airport was. They said it was Geneva and the ticket was about €100. I asked him how far €47 would get me and they said about halfway. I handed over the money and got onto the bus hoping that they would forget me. This worked for a while but at one of the stops they remembered me and chucked me off. There I am, standing on the side of the road and I've got fuck all and I don't know where I am.

I wandered around for a bit and went into a shop to do a bit of survival shoplifting, then I wandered around a bit more hoping to catch a lift from somewhere. I was lucky again and I managed to get a couple of lifts that basically got me almost to Geneva airport. I walked the rest of the way and on arrival gave the staff him a load of old crap about doing a survival exercise and being dropped off and told to make my way back. I had to talk to several people then a manager of some sort, then his manager and then someone else's manager. Unbelievably, I managed to blag a flight back to the UK, but the problem was the flight was going to Leeds and I had to be in Bulford in Wiltshire by Monday morning.

I landed in Leeds early morning on the Sunday and phoned my dad reversing the charges. "Hey Dad! Any chance you can pick me up from Leeds airport?"

The poor bastard had just done a full days work and had to go from Stoke-on-Trent to fetch me from Leeds. Don't you just love Dads? Whatever shit we get up to they did it thirty years ago, so no explanation needed and no "Well you have no one to blame but yourself!". Then he drove me all the way to Bulford, drove back to Stoke-on-Trent and went straight back to work. (Thanks Dad!) I once read somewhere that 'No good deed goes unpunished' and this was certainly the case with him. As well as doing a day's work, driving me to Bulford and then going straight back to another day's work without any sleep, on the way down south I managed to break two of his fingers when I accidentally slammed the car door on him. It did work out quite well though, because every time he started to doze off I would flick his finger and that would wake him back up again.

I arrived back in Bulford camp about 7:30 pm on Sunday, had a shower, got changed and went to the NAAFI to buy a crate of beer. I then went to the common room and dragged a sofa out and took it down to the MT sheds where the coach was due to arrive with the rest of my unit on it. There I lounged, sipping a cold one.

I managed to drink nearly the entire crate by the time the coach pulled up literally in front of me, at which point I gave them a very drunk greeting and said, "Hey lads you took your fucking time didn't you?"

To make it even better, it turned out that it was possibly the worst coach trip ever. They'd been stuck in traffic for four hours with one toilet on the coach and all these blokes were getting hot and pissed off while I'm sat there on a comfy sofa with a beer induced smile on my face. The 2 i/c got off the coach and stopped dead when he saw me. He just said, "You lucky bastard".

Lance Corporal Peter Djuro Tideswell

A shit day

One day I was driving the OC as he wanted to come on some of my detachment visits, and I was the only technician Sergeant in the Squadron at the time when there should have been four – see, there's always been manpower shortages, we just had hundreds more units. Anyhow, Major Brown, (or Phil to his running mates. I wasn't one of his running mates, so Sir to me), was in the passenger seat as we approached a trunk node command location at about 04:00. We approached the location and the interesting individual George Harrison popped out and waved us to a halt. He leant into the window of the rover and issued the first part of the daily password and I responded correctly. "Morning Sarge, good job you got that right or you wouldn't be coming in….. Oh morning Boss man, sorry didn't see you there in the dark with cam cream on, good job!"
"Morning Sig Harrison, everything OK?" said the OC.
"I know I'm being kicked out, but I'm still one of the best soldiers here sir, I didn't desert my post when I asked node command for a relief and none came, so I've shat my pants instead!"
"Pardon?"
George patiently explained. "I had to just shit in me pants sir, they didn't send me a relief." With this he sticks his hand into the back of his combats and pulls out a finger with shit on it. Fair enough George, point proved. He then wiped his fingers clean on the side of where the guard is supposed to be concealed whilst chatting happily, "When you go in, can you get someone to relieve me so I can go and clean up?".
We sorted a relief for George and fifteen minutes later when we went into the admin area to grab a brew we found George standing bollock naked with a wash bowl on one of the benches and one foot on the G1098 table. It was wobbling all over, and so was he, dripping shitty water all over the admin location.

We returned three hours later after we had visited some of the outlying detachments to do some repairs and decided to grab some scoff before moving on. I went into the repair vehicle (techs exercise haven) for a decent coffee and a chat with my mate Gez. This vehicle has air conditioning units because some of our equipment is quite sensitive so it's usually cool and sweet smelling in there. This time it literally smelt like shit. And not cow shit, or horse shit, which you would recognise, but human shit. "Fucking hell it stinks in here Gez." says I.
"It's the pig farm." said Gez, "They always smell like shit."
It hadn't smelt like that outside though, so I turned on the other ACU and it blew fresh smelling air. "You've got something up with that ACU Gez, is it next to the barn extractor or something?"
"I don't think so," he said. "I'll check." He went outside and was back moments later. "Dirty fucking bastards!" he raved.
George had stretched his shitty pants over the air conditioning input vents to dry them. He hadn't attempted to clean them; they were totally encrusted.
We also had a lad nicknamed Suicide Sid who kept trying to top himself. One day he tried to put the gate guards weapon in his mouth, and cock it so he could blow his own head off, but the guard was wearing the weapon slung across his chest and he moved away quickly breaking off several of Sid's front teeth. Sid was left screaming in pain as all the nerves had been exposed. His final attempt that we know of was when he went onto the roof of the block late at night and jumped off. What Sid didn't know was that the Squadron had set up a bouncy castle for an open day starting the next morning. He couldn't see it in the dark, but he bounced off it and broke both of his legs – we didn't hear of him after that.

Gaz Duffy, Royal Signals (1985-2010)

Another great idea...

During the mid-eighties a certain RE Field Squadron were tasked with running a two-week Adventure camp for squaddie brats. This was to be at a location in the Harz mountains, home of the British Army winter sports camp, which was housed in an old castle up a mountain.
Our small, tented camp was well outside the main one and was positioned at the foot of the mountain by the Dams. So we arrived, set up a tented camp, made our acquaintance with the local Hofmeister, and waited for the arrival of the said brats!
The first week was for under fourteens, followed in the second week by over fourteens. Loads of activities going on for these little darlings, rock climbing, abseiling, canoeing, and other things to keep them amused.
Come the middle weekend we were given some time off, so all eager for a beer or two... who am I kidding, we sank the local town! Hence the singing of the song 'A pub with no beer', especially when the British Army were in town.
So the night went on past late and into the early hours, and the transport that had been arranged to pick us up arrived.
I don't remember who, but it was at this point that one of us had a great idea. We decided to load the back of the four tonner with the local window boxes which all had lovely flower arrangements in them, the type you see on many windows up and down the Strasse. The plan was to make the tentage area a bit more decorative so yours truly was up the back of the four tonner, helping to load them up and when we seemed to have enough everyone climbed on board and off we went back to camp. The drive was about twenty minutes or so, so I found a nice soft pile of canvas tent bags up the front and curled up between a couple. Zzzzzzzzzz.......
Unsurprisingly, our nocturnal antics had been noticed by the locals. Maybe, just maybe, we weren't as quiet as we thought

when we drunk-as-a-skunk squaddies loaded heavy mud filled boxes onto the back of a noisy lorry. Anyway, the driver was pulled over by the local Polizei who escorted the truck and flower boxes back to town whereupon all the boxes were replaced.

Then the lovely German police escorted the truck up the mountain to the winter sports camp at the castle, the guys were handed over to the guard, and the Camp Commandant was called out. He was not a happy chappy. He ordered the lads inside, but fortunately for me I was *not* ordered inside. No dear reader, I was still up at the front of the four tonner fast asleep.

In the morning I woke up from a really good kip and freshened up as best I could with a couple of handfuls of water from a jerrycan beside my pile of tents. (Does wonders.) I rolled out of the back of the truck and saw the main camp gates just ahead of me, so I made my way through them with a cheery, "Good morning!" to the guard as I passed through and started the long walk back down the mountain to our tents.

Later that morning I was joined by the rest of the party who were amazed that I did not get caught because I normally snore very loudly. "Well," said I, "maybe because I had a mouth full of canvas."

Oh, how I'd go back in time to do it all again......

A-J ACC Attached to 21 Engineer Regiment. BFPO 48.

The throne room

During the first gulf war our OP was attached to the QRIH (tankies) and several WRACs visited their position to see how the guys were preparing for coming operation. At one point during the visit a certain Gunner (no it wasn't me) noticed a queue of WRACs leading to a square of hessian, held up by four poles, right in the centre of the circled vehicles. On closer inspection, said Gunner came to realise this was a toilet being used by the female soldiers and was an infinitely better option that the usual shovel recce into the dark desert when nature came calling. After the WRACs had departed, the Gunner walked over to the square and saw it contained a varnished wooden box with a hole in the top, a toilet seat and of course, the QRIH regimental crest on the front.

"Blinding!" thinks the Gunner and parks his arse on the toilet completely unaware he's been spotted, and more importantly by who. All of a sudden the relaxed soldier hears, "What the fuck is a Gunner doing on the Colonel's toilet?" and through a gap in the hessian sees the QRIH RSM hurtling towards him, pace stick in hand.

Rapidly, the Gunner donned his trousers and stood facing the apoplectic, red faced, warrant officer. Within seconds of arriving the poor Gunner was marched across the position and ordered to re-dig the 'Fucking Colonel's toilet' on a spot marked X in the sand by the RSM's shiny wooden brass tipped stick... and of course, the hessian then had to be reassembled, all in the blazing heat while being observed by a highly amused audience of QRIH Troopers. Long story short, don't use a Cavalry Officers throne unless you are absolutely sure his RSM is not about!!

Gunner 'X' RA

"A man who is good enough to shed his blood for the country is good enough to be given a great deal afterward. "
Theodore Roosevelt

Sod this, I'm going home.

Editors note – This is a story that I have been trying to track down for years, and I have finally found someone who was there! Its important to know for context that 16 Air Defence Regiment RA was predominantly Scottish and had something of a wild reputation.

I think it was in 1982 or 1983, I can't remember now, (It was 1981 – Jonno DP) I was in West Riding barracks, Dortmund with 16 Air Defence Regiment and one weekend one of our blokes made an alcohol induced decision to go home to Blighty despite having no leave and no money. In those days Bedford POD vehicles (fuel tankers) always had the keys left in the ignition in case they needed to be moved in an emergency. Thinking that with two huge fuel tanks on the back refuelling wouldn't be a problem, he got in and off he went. In fact, the POD that he was in carried petrol in the tanks on the back, and Bedfords ran on diesel, but plans created in the battery bar aren't usually criminal masterpieces are they?

He started the POD up and then drove off to the gate manned by 26 Field Regiment (we shared the barracks with them) and seeing an approaching army vehicle they assumed it was legit and raised the barrier to let him through. One of ours had seen what had happened though, and the RMP and GCP were informed and he soon found himself with lots of blue lights in his rear view mirrors.

Now PODs are really heavy and do about 30mph flat out. Also, they don't have power steering (well they didn't then anyway) so escaping from a souped up GCP vehicle was a bit much to ask. Even an RMP landrover feels like a Ferrari by comparison, so it can't have been much of a chase, but it ended with him running a red light, turning the POD over and causing an explosion in the middle of Dortmund, setting fire to a shop and causing an estimated $650,000 worth of damage. He legged it from the scene but handed himself in a few hours later. My memory may be wrong after forty years, but I think this guy was headquarters battery, a really quiet gunner normally.

The Germans were so angry about this that ended up insisting that the entire regiment get sent back to the UK. About 6 months after the incident we were gone, back to Kirton Linsey. Apparently, one of the reasons the Germans wanted us gone so quick was because we had a bit of a reputation for being slightly bonkers Scotsmen. The irony of this story is that the guy who blew up the centre of Dortmund with a POD was a bloody Englishman! I might be wrong but I don't think 16 regiment ever went back to Germany.

This incident enhanced our reputation as chief arsonists in BAOR as there had been another incident in 1975.

We were stationed in Soest then and we had a new NAAFI manager posted in. So what? Well, this guy was a complete asshole and one day he seriously pissed off two of our lads, and I mean *seriously*. He lived in a flat at the back of the NAAFI and had his camper bus, his pride and joy, parked out the front. Our two blokes, Jim and Amos, drunk of course, decided to get revenge by torching his bus. This was quickly noticed by half the battery as our accommodation was the other side of the road. One of them was siphoning the tank, and the other one had a basin on his head for some reason. The attempt to siphon fuel out of the tank to help get the fire started, was doomed to failure though. They didn't realise it was a diesel engine and diesel is very hard to light.

Eventually they got a fire going but being hammered were quickly caught and ended up doing two years nick before being kicked out.

Blackie 16 Air Defence Regiment Royal Artillery

Pretty fucking Polly

My last ship was HMS Active, a type 21 frigate, and I was lucky enough to be on it in 1993 when it was sent to do a six month deployment to the Caribbean, something called the West Indies Guard ship. All the type 21 Frigates took it in turns to do this, and now it was our go! On the previous trip four years ago a lady had come on board and had given the ship a baby African Grey parrot called Jenny as a present. For the first four years of its life it lived in the Stokers mess and they would look after it, feed it and clean the cage. One of the lads, MEM Jones, used to walk around the ship with Jenny on his shoulder.

After four years the stokers decided that it was someone elses turn to look after the parrot because if no one in the stokers mess wanted to clean the cage out it started to get a bit smelly, and if you were trying to get some sleep it would often squawk loudly and wake you up, so they started looking around for another mess willing to take it on. A notice was put on orders saying that they were looking for a new home for Jenny and would any of the messes like to have their own pet parrot, but over the years they had told everyone that it was a pain in the ass, so there were no takers. In the end the marine engineering officer, a lieutenant commander, decided that the officers had to do the right thing and give Jenny a new home in their wardroom. This made sense, because as officers we all had our own cabins as well as the actual mess so the parrot could live there and not disturb anyone. Brilliant!

Often whilst we were in the West Indies we would have cocktail parties and the consulate would be responsible for sending out invitations to the local dignitaries inviting them to come on board. And we young officers were briefed that a cocktail party would last about two hours and you shouldn't talk to the same person the whole time, the captain would always be floating past muttering, "Mingle mingle, mingle, young man." You were also reminded that we should always make a good impression and leave them thinking what a wonderful thing the Royal Navy is and that we were all charming young men and pillars of virtue.

In reality you would start with the older guests and make your way towards the good looking girls at the end. The plan was that after the cocktail party had finished you would say to the young ladies that if they would like to continue the conversation you would like to invite them down to the wardroom so that we can spend more time together. Sometimes it worked, and sometimes it didn't, so much for virtue.

The weapons engineering officer was a lovely man called Peter Mills and he'd been in quite a few years so was a lot older than the rest of us. He was married to Deacon, so he was very religious and had no intentions to take young totty down to the wardroom to try it on, but instead he would take people who interested him down there. This particular time he took down a very posh lady and her equally posh husband, both of whom spoke with extremely plummy accents. So there were all the young officers in the wardroom trying to get our guests tipsy and try our luck when in walks Peter with this extremely elegant lady and her husband. As she walked in she saw the parrot and trilled, "Ooh! An African Grey! How lovely! How delightful!" She walked across to the parrot cooing at it and saying how lovely it was whilst we looked on with our best fake smiles.

Jenny the parrot, however, was not quite so polite as she was. She'd spent four years sharing a space with somewhat more uncouth stokers, so she regarded the posh lady with a beady eye for a moment, and then just squawked in a very loud voice, "FUCK OFF!!!"

There was a momentary stunned silence before our lady guests roared with laughter, and it was nearly impossible for us to keep a straight face. Poor Peter started apologising and kept apologising his guests out of the door. For all I know, he is still apologising to them now.

On reflection we should have thought about this because stokers have many qualities, but refined and polite conversation was not one of them. In fact they swear like absolute troopers. It got to the point with Jenny that whenever we had any guests on board we had to hide her in the first lieutenants cabin. Ah well, life in a blue suit.

Sub Lieutenant Jonathan Cantelo Jones. Royal Navy

The Unknown Soldier

Whilst serving as a chaplain on the Western Front in 1916 Reverend David Railton saw a grave marked by a rough cross which bore the words 'An Unknown British Soldier' and he had an idea that would spread around the world. There were around 200,000 British combatants recorded as missing after this conflict and the families therefore had no final resting place on which to focus their grief. It was the intention after World War I that all relatives of combatants whose bodies had not been identified, could believe that the unknown warrior could be their lost husband, father, brother, or son.

After the war he suggested an unidentified British combatant be removed from a temporary grave on the Western Front and be reburied with full ceremonial to honour the dead and give a focus for those who had lost a loved one. The idea received a wave of public support and the backing of the Dean of Westminster, the Prime Minister David Lloyd George, and King George V. At around the same time a similar idea arose in France and immediately received widespread support.

On November the 7th 1920, in the utmost secrecy, the bodies of four (some accounts say six) unidentified British soldiers were exhumed from temporary cemeteries where the British had engaged in major battles. Even the soldiers doing the exhumation were not told why. The bodies were taken to GHQ at St-Pol-Sur-Ternoise, near Arras, and there the commander of British forces in France and Flanders, Brigadier-General Wyatt, selected one body at random and an honour guard stood overnight. The other bodies were reburied in a British war cemetery.

On the 9th of November the Unknown Warrior was transferred under guard, with troops lining the route, to the medieval castle within the ancient citadel at Boulogne. For the occasion the castle library was transformed into a chapelle ardente (a room where a sovereign lies in state before burial) and a company from the French 8th Infantry Regiment, recently awarded the Légion d'Honneur en masse, stood vigil overnight. The next morning a coffin made of oak from a tree that had grown in the grounds of Hampton Court was brought and the unknown warrior was placed inside, the coffin then being sealed shut with iron bands. A crusaders sword and a shield inscribed with the words 'A British Warrior who fell in the Great War 1914-1918 for king and country' was attached to the lid, items that had been chosen personally from the Royal collection by King George V. Then it was draped with the union flag that Reverend Railton had used as an altar cloth whilst giving services on the Western Front.

The coffin was placed onto a French military wagon drawn by six black horses and at 10:30 a.m. all the church bells of Boulogne rang a lament whilst the massed trumpets of the French cavalry and the bugles of the French infantry played Aux Champs which is the French equivalent of the Last Post. Then the mile-long procession led by one thousand local schoolchildren and escorted by a division of French troops, made its way down to the harbour.

At the quayside Marshal Foch, who had been the Western Fronts supreme allied commander during the war, saluted the casket before it was carried up the gangway of the destroyer HMS Verdun and it was piped aboard with an admirals call. The Verdun slipped anchor just before noon and was joined by an escort of six battleships. As the flotilla approached Dover Castle it received a nineteen gun salute, normally only given for the prime minister, field marshals, and admirals of the fleet, and then travelled by special train to Victoria Station where it arrived at platform 8 that evening and remained overnight. A plaque at Victoria Station marks the spot and every year on 10 November a small remembrance service, organised by The Western Front Association, takes place there.

On the morning of the 11th of November 1920, the second anniversary of the armistice, the casket was placed onto a gun carriage of N Battery Royal Horse Artillery and was drawn by six black horses through immense and silent crowds. As the cortege set off, another nineteen gun salute was fired in Hyde Park and it went to Whitehall where the Cenotaph was unveiled by the King, followed by a two minute silence at 11am. (A cenotaph is a symbolic empty tomb to honour someone who's remains are elsewhere.) The gun carriage was then followed by The King, the Royal Family and ministers of state to Westminster Abbey, where the casket was carried into the West Nave flanked by a guard of honour of one hundred recipients of the Victoria Cross. Every recipient of the Victoria cross held their hands, not over their heart, but over their medals, hiding them in recognition that their deeds of valour were insignificant compared to those who had laid down their lives.

The guests of honour were a group of about one hundred women who had been chosen because they had each lost their husband and all their sons in the war. Every such woman who had applied for a place got it.

As this ceremony was taking place a similar one was happening in France to honour their Unknown Warrior, but the actual interment took place in the Arc de Triomphe the following January.

Only a few feet inside the entrance to the Abbey, the Unknown Warrior was placed in his tomb where he remains to this day, and his grave was filled in using 100 sandbags of earth from the battlefields of the First World War. The grave was then capped with a slab of black Belgian marble. Servicemen from the armed forces stood guard as an estimated one and a quarter million mourners filed silently past, an event which seems to have acted as a catharsis for the nation for the dreadful losses sustained in the conflict.

Other countries adopted the idea, and today there are tombs containing an unknown soldier in almost sixty countries, some having multiple 'Unknown Soldiers', (America has five, Japan has four and Iran has three for example). Some countries also have tombs for an unknown Sailor.

Today the original Tomb of the Unknown Soldier is one of the most visited war graves in the world. In a time when wars engaged in by western forces have casualty lists in the hundreds or low thousands, the statistics from the First World War are hard to visualise but try this. If all the British Empires dead of the First World War were to march past you in three ranks it would take them about five days and nights.

If you visit Westminster Abbey you will see that there are grave slabs covering the floor marking the final resting place of hundreds of people, many of them famous even today. But as a mark of enduring respect no one, and that includes the reigning monarch, *ever* walks across the tomb of the unknown soldier. When the Duke of York, later King George VI and father to Queen Elizabeth II, married Lady Elizabeth Bowes Lyons in the Abbey in 1923 she left her wedding bouquet on the tomb as a mark of respect as she had lost her brother Fergus at the Battle of Loos in 1915. Since then, all royal brides married in the Abbey have sent back their bouquets to be laid on the grave, and before she died in 2002 Queen Elizabeth the Queen Mother expressed the wish for her funeral wreath to be placed on the Tomb of the Unknown Warrior. Her daughter, Queen Elizabeth II personally fulfilled this wish the day after the funeral.

A year after the burial the unknown warrior was given the United States' highest award for valour, the Medal of Honor, from the hand of General John Pershing and it hangs on a pillar close to the tomb. Shortly afterward the American Unknown Soldier was reciprocally awarded the Victoria Cross.

The text inscribed on the tomb is taken from the bible 'They buried him among the kings, because he had done good toward God and toward his house'.

Researched and written by Jonno DP.

Well, that's the end of book 3, I hope you enjoyed reading it as much as I did writing it, and once again thank all the people who sent me stories or who had me phone them. Great fun.

If a memory of yours has been woken from its slumber by this book and you have a tale with something interesting, dangerous or disgusting (or preferably all three) please email it to me at damonjohnson@zoho.com and your immortality will be assured by appearing in book 4!! If you prefer you can email me your phone number and I will give you a ring, or a third option is to get hold of me via Facebook. I am the Damon Johnson with a photo of me in the middle distance on some steps. Thanks by the way to all the people who sent me a friend request, if they are ex forces I always accept it, and it has made me feel much more popular than I actually am.

At the time of writing this I have about a third of the material needed for another book, so room for more!

According to the reviews on the Amazon website these books give a lot of laughs to people with that *special* sense of humour so please go there and leave some stars so it's more visible in searches for things like 'Military' or 'Cold War', and if you want to leave a review, that's even better, these reviews are read by me with great interest. I am chucking out about one book every 18 months whilst working full time (It takes ages to do a book, much longer than you would think) and I would like to produce many more before we all die.

If you want to know when the next book is out you can click on 'follow author' on the Amazon page for any of the books and you will be automatically notified when its published, so I am told, I have no idea how these things work.

And now I am going to make an egg banjo and a NATO brew, swing a lamp and pull up a sandbag. I might even get into a maggot and have some gonk. See you in book 4 sicko!

Glossary

2i/c. 2nd in command.

5's and 20's. This is an Iraq/Afghanistan-ism. Due to the high threat of IEDs. Whenever you stopped on a patrol you'd check your immediate five metre surroundings. If you were staying in position for more than a few minutes you'd expand to twenty metres, using optics to assist. It's now colloquially known as a synonym for checking for threats in any environment - including Civ Div, I.E. "I was about to tell this dirty joke and had to do a quick 5s and 20s in case some granny was nearby."

5th Skins. The 5th Inskilling Dragoon Guards. Known colloquially as the 5th skins, or if you didn't like them, the foreskins.

ACC. Army Catering Corps. AKA slop jockeys or cabbage mechanics. To be fair, they were pretty good, we just made sure they didn't hear it from us.

Ack. Assistant.

AD. Air Defence

ADSR. Armoured Division HQ & Signal Regiment.

AK47. Standard issue rifle for eastern European armies.

Arty Limber. The truck that carries ammunition for an artillery gun, and with towed artillery, rather than self-propelled, may tow the gun as well.

BATUS. British Army Training Unit Suffield. A huge (and I do mean HUGE) training area in Canada. Pro tip – don't go digging there. Everyone and his uncle have buried ammunition there by the ton.

BC. Battery Commander.

Bedford. 4 ton general purpose truck.

BFBS/SSVC. British Forces Broadcasting Service (Forces TV and Radio) and Services Sound and Vision Corporation (Forces Cinema).

Biff chit. A derogatory term for a sick chit/medical note that excuses someone from various types of military work or exercise.

BLS. Basic Life Support. Later changed to BCD, Battlefield Casualty Drills.

BMH. British Military Hospital.

Bombardier. Two stripe NCO in the Artillery/Horse Artillery. Known as a Corporal in the rest of the army.

Bratties mit pommes. Bratwurst and chips.

Bundesbahn. German railway.

Casevac. Casualty evacuation

C in C. Commander in Chief

Civ Div. Civilians.

Colonel Gaddafi. NAAFI.

Comcen. Communication Centre.

CP. Command Post.

DF. Direction Finding.

Don 10. Cable connecting one talky thing to another talky thing.

DS. Directing Staff. The people in charge of an exercise or activity.

E&E exercise. Escape and Evasion exercise. Grown up version of hide and seek. Well, not always *that* grown up.

Endex. End of Exercise.

FLRT. Fork Lift Rough Terrain.

FOO. Forward Observation Officer.

GCP. German Civil Police.

Gun sub. One artillery gun out of a battery of guns.

ICBM. Intercontinental Ballistic Missile. These are the nightmare things that can end the world in a couple of hours. About a hundred foot long, weighing 150 tons, a range of ten thousand miles or so, multiple warheads and the explosive power of about 95 Hiroshima bombs. And there are thousands of these things in existence right now.

i/c. In command of/In charge of.

IED. Improvised Explosive Device.

Jankers. A punishment that meant doing shitty jobs in the evening and weekends whilst being paraded several times a day to increase the fuck-around-factor. Later known as ROP's (Restriction Of Privileges) or ropes.

JRC. Junior Ranks Club.

Juniors. Junior Leaders.

LAD. Light Aid Detachment. The REME mechanics that are with a regiment as the first line of repair.

Liney. Royal Signals linesmen.

Maggot. Sleeping bag. So called because unrolled they looked like huge maggots. Often very old and thin. I could actually see through mine. Sleep well lads.

Monkeys. See MP.

MP. Military Police, AKA Royal Military Police, AKA Monkeys, AKA Redcaps, AKA complete bastards. In wartime they would briefly direct military traffic before being shot by their own side.

MT. Motor Transport.

NBC. Nuclear, Chemical, Biological. When I got a bit of experience, I asked how these suits protect against nuclear attacks. Obviously, a thin green suit with a charcoal lining wouldn't protect against a nuclear blast, but what about radiation that needs several inches of lead to stop it. I was told it does nothing to protect against radiation. Oh ta. What about biological attack? Nope. The bacteria wouldn't be stopped by the suit or the respirator. But at least they protect from chemical attack, right? Yes, but only if you are wearing several layers of clothing. Oh wonderful, thanks a lot Q.

NCO. Non-Commissioned Officer. Anyone above the rank of private, but below the rank of commissioned officer. Junior NCOs (JNCO) are Lance Corporals and Corporals, Senior NCO's (SNCO) are Sergeants, Staff Sergeants and Sergeant Majors.

NI. Northern Ireland.

Noch zwei biers. Another two beers.

Noddy suits. See NBC suits.

No duff. This means a message is genuine, rather than for the purposes of the exercise. For example, if you transmitted a message saying you had taken casualties on an exercise it would be assumed you hadn't really. If you prefixed the message with 'No duff' then you are telling the receiving station that you really do have casualties.

OC. Officer Commanding.

OP. Observation post.

Ord. Ordnance.

Pace stick. A wooden stick usually topped with silver or brass carried by various types of bastard.

Pit. Bed.

POD. Petrol, Oil, Dispenser. A small tanker modified from a four ton lorry.

P.O.L. Petrol, Oil, and Lubricants.

QRF. Quick Reaction Force.

QRIH. Queens Royal Irish Hussars.

RA. Royal Artillery.

Rasman. See RSM.

RGJ. Royal Green Jackets. AKA the Black Mafia. Nutters. Don't fuck with them.

RE. Royal Engineers.

REME. Royal Electrical and Mechanical Engineers. Or Ruin Everything Mechanical Eventually.

Recy mech/reccer mech. The army version of the AA. If you ever watch a big military convoy go by the last bit will be REME and the very last bit will be a weird looking vehicle crewed by weird looking soldiers. This is to recover any broken-down vehicles. A strange but interesting group of people.

RHA. Royal Horse Artillery. Basically the same tasks as Royal Artillery, but they tend to be very old regiments. The 'Horse' part refers to the fact that they used to support cavalry.

Rodney. Derogatory term for an officer. We also used to call them Ruperts.

RRF. Royal Regiment of Fusiliers.

RSM. Regimental Sergeant Major. The most senior Non-Commissioned Officer in a unit. A man to be feared, and if possible avoided.

RTR. Royal Tank Regiment.

Rupert. See Rodney.

Schnellie. Short for schnellimbiss. A German fast-food establishment similar to a British chip shop.

Shanksies pony. Walking.

SIB. Special Investigation Branch. The Military Police version of civilian CID.

Sigcen. Signals centre.

Siggy. Signaller.

Stalwart. A six wheeled, petrol engined, boat shaped, semi armoured truck used to carry ammunition and fuel for front line regiments. YouTube them, they are sexy bastards.

SOP. Standard Operating Proceedure.

Stag. Guard duty/sentry duty.

SNCO. Senior NCO. See NCO.

Stadt. German word for city or city centre.

SSM. Surface to Surface Missile or Squadron Sergeant Major. Quite easy to tell apart. One is a fast moving object that can explode when you are not expecting it, and the other one is a surface to surface missile.

SQMS. Squadron Quartermaster Sergeant.

TA. Territorial Army.

UKLF. United Kingdom Land Forces.

UVF. Ulster Volunteer Force.

VCP. Vehicle Check Point.

VOR. Vehicle Off Road. A vehicle that cannot be used due to a major fault.

Walkman. 1980s portable music device. It was crap. It took only one cassette and was powered by AA batteries. Did we really buy this shit?

WO. Warrant Officer. (AKA Sergeant Major, the shouty one who always seems to be angry about something.)

WRAC. Women's Royal Army Corps, or Warm Round And Cuddly. There were other versions of the letters WRAC, but I am not saying.

If you enjoyed this book, I recommend this one by Harry Clacy...

Harry was a Crap Hat - (Second Edition) At the age of sixteen I joined the British Army with every intention of winning a Victoria Cross for saving my unit from certain death...

Or this one is pretty good…

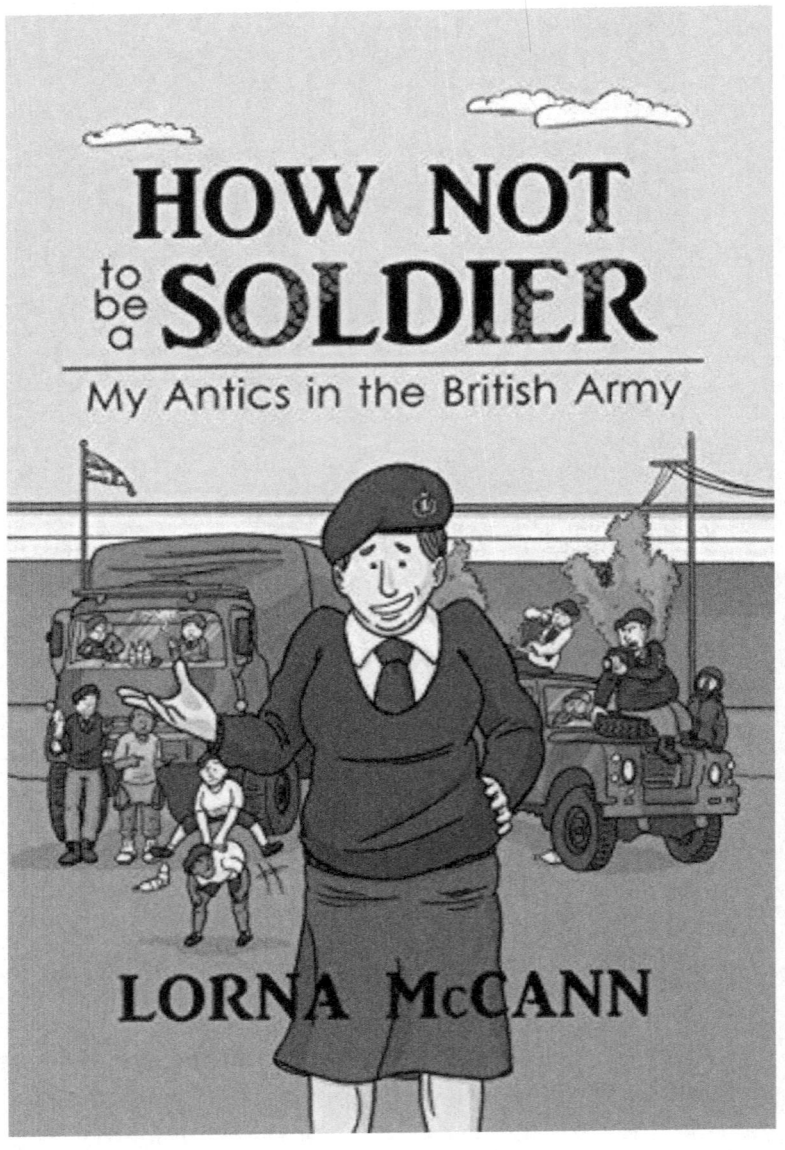

HOW NOT to be a SOLDIER

My Antics in the British Army

LORNA McCANN

Seeing life from the perspective of a female soldier was interesting and often very funny.

Or if you want something more up to date...

GARRY PATON

TO KUWAIT AND BACK

The Story of a Tank Troop

Printed in Great Britain
by Amazon